Hired@Home

The Christian Mother's Guide to Working From Home

Hired@Home

The Christian Mother's Guide to Working From Home

SARAH HAMAKER

DPL
PRESS

Los Angeles

Hired@Home: The Christian Mother's Guide to Working From Home

PRINTED IN THE UNITED STATES OF AMERICA

Cover Design: Jeremy Hunt, *www.SDMFX.com*

Author Photo: Copyright Donna Hamaker

For information regarding special discounts for bulk purchases and or corporate branding, please contact:

DPL Press, Inc., P.O. Box 2135, Los Angeles, CA 90723; Special Sales: 800-550-3502. Visit us at *DPLPress.com.*

Library of Congress Cataloging-in-Publication Data
Information Available by Request from Publisher

Scripture quotations are taken from the Holy Bible, New Living Translation, copyright 1996. Used by permission of Tyndale House Publishers, Inc., Wheaton, Illinois 60189. All rights reserved.

ISBN-13: 978 09760791-9-4

1   2   3   4   5   6   7   8   9   10

Table of Contents

Introduction

So you want to work from home. There has never been a better time to do so, and the number of women who work at home is on the rise.[1] Technological advances, such as personal computers, the Internet, and email, have opened up at-home job opportunities our mothers and grandmothers never dreamed possible.

Women are finding a balance between at-home work[2], household duties, and caring for children, as the authors of *What's a Smart Woman Like You Doing At Home?* discovered:

"Women who desire to keep up career skills, or even embark on totally new endeavors, are doing so with admirable creativity while remaining mothers at home.

"Home businesses are one way many mothers have solved the problem of bringing in an income or keeping up talents while staying home with their children."[3]

Mothers who work are no longer the exception. More than half the nation's eighty million mothers between the ages of fifteen and forty-four work part-time or full time, according to data from the U.S. government.[4] In addition, many of the 5.6 million moms who stay home full time with young children are likely to work at some point in either paid or unpaid (volunteer) employment.[5] A May 2005 *Washington Post* study found that of the thirty-six percent of moms in the poll who describe themselves as stay-at-home, twenty-six percent do some sort of work for pay from home.[6]

Working women have transformed their at-the-office employment into at-home work opportunities. Other women tap into their creative side and launch successful small businesses. Women running at-home businesses are making good money—some have annual sales in the $100,000 range or even in the millions.[7]

But these aren't just your grandmother's at-home businesses. In a 1971 book about careers at home, the dominant choices revolved around crafts, such as candle making, dressmaking, making party favors, toy making, and constructing wall shadow boxes, to name just a few.

These crafts are still viable options today. But the 1970s stay-at-home mother without the artistic skills required for many of these crafts faced limited choices—especially since non-craft at-home jobs, such as bookkeeping, childcare, mail-order selling, translating, typing, and writing, required a skill set she may not have possessed.[8]

Today, a mom can do just about anything from home. Mom entrepreneurs have started businesses as at-home advertisers, authors, attorneys and alpaca raisers; bakers and beauty consultants; chefs, cleaners and crossword puzzle makers; dress, diaper and decal designers; educational therapists and engineers; financial planners, fitness trainers and furniture designers; genealogists and graphic designers; home decorators, information specialists and inventors; jewelry makers, lifestyle coaches, marketers, news producers and nurses; organizers, painters, pet sitters, potty trainers and private investigators; quilt makers, real estate agents, singers, skin-care specialists and speech therapists; taxidermists, T-shirt designers and toy-makers; virtual assistants, Web designers, wedding planners and writers.[9]

The face of small businesses—many of which are home-based—is changing, too, according to a recent Intuit-sponsored study from the Institute for the Future.[10]

The Intuit study found that, over the next decade, women will continue to start their own businesses, many of those from home. As a dual-income society, many women have to balance work and home life. To ease that stress, "Mompreneurs" start businesses to gain flexibility. These women develop good networks and find success through teamwork and the support of other mompreneurs.

Recent books about women and working also comment on the viability of at-home employment. In her book *7 Myths of Working Mothers*, Suzanne Venker talks about the at-home mother. "Just because a mother doesn't pursue a full-fledged career—complete with time clock, commute, and nearby daycare facility—doesn't mean she's out of the job market."[11]

Venker found that the common thread for women who work part-time or have flexible work schedules is their desire to work around their children's schedules. Working from home often helps them fulfill that need.

Christian authors also see the viability of mothers working from home. The late Christian author and financial adviser Larry Burkett, in his book *Women Leaving the Workplace*, wrote how stay-at-home mothers also can fit work into their home schedules: "Leaving the formal marketplace to be a stay-at-home mother does not necessarily mean giving up all additional income. In fact, for many women just the opposite has proved to be true. Working at home, they are able to create cottage-industry jobs that match or even increase their previous net incomes."[12]

Burkett also wrote of the many opportunities available to stay-at-home moms: "Just as the transfer of traditional office work has benefited companies and their employees, it also has spawned whole new opportunities for full-time moms.... Totally removed from the traditional business environment, other home-based businesses have developed over the last several decades whose economic impact is beginning to rival the retail stores."[13]

What makes these women different is their desire to be home with their children and to work from home, too. In my interviews with stay-at-home mothers who also work from home, all of them said part of the reason they do it is because they want to be home with their children. Or, as Venker puts it, "It never seems to have occurred to feminists that perhaps women don't want to compete in the business world because they want to be mothers, first and foremost."[14] Flex-time, part-time, and job sharing, along with a husband's willingness to help with more housework, provide more avenues for work opportunities for women today.

Working from home provides an outlet for a woman's creativity, allows her to use her God-given talents and abilities, gives her the means to help her family's finances, and permits her to share her skills with her family, friends, and community.

As Betsy Hart, a single mother of four who works from her Chicago home, says, "I really think that we as women need to look for things that will take us outside the home intellectually, to do something that is not about our children.

Historically, there was so much physical work to be done in the home. In modern times, with the work of maintaining a home so much less time-consuming, we moms have opportunities to work outside our home or from our home. What a wonderful thing. I think that children need to see that work is good, and that we mothers have other things out in the world besides them."

Our Stories

In this book, you will meet Christian women from all over the United States who are working from home in many different and diverse fields and occupations: women like Dixie Moore, who teaches children's knitting classes; Lisa Harmon, who does her office manager job mostly from home; Lori Boyd Schantz, a senior scientist; Martha Leone, a graphic designer; Tami Conklin, a math tutor; Jenny Annoni, a computer network engineer; Paula Sokody Wilding, an online teacher; Toni Lane, a breast-feeding counselor; Debbie Hufford, a seamstress; Elizabeth Anne Tappan, a medical transcriptionist; Jennifer Coffin, a potter; Melanie Dobson, a novelist; Tina Simpson, a missionary recruiter; Tonya Travelstead, a piano teacher; and Jennifer Clauson, an Internet bookseller.

I, too, work from home as a freelance writer and editor, and have done so since my oldest child was barely two months old. Like some of the women I interviewed for this book, my at-home career began out of necessity.

While pregnant with our first child, I worked as a writer and editor for a national trade association in Washington, D.C. I was planning to quit my job a week before the due date, but then we found out my husband would be laid off from his job a month before the birth.

Two months into my leave, the association asked me to work on two major projects from home, which I did. When my husband found a job a scant three weeks before my leave was up (talk about God's timing!), I was able to tender my resignation and continue working on the projects as a freelancer.

I have gradually added more clients and children through the years. I now have a five-year-old, a three-year-old, and a sixteen-month-old.

I generally work between seven and twenty hours a week, sometimes more, depending on deadlines and assignments—all without regular childcare.

I've made business calls with my children hollering in the other room (thank goodness for telephone headsets with mute buttons), worked late at night to finish a project, and taken my laptop to the porch while the children played outside.

I'm thankful that I have a profession that so easily transfers to at-home work. However, in talking to other stay-at-home moms, I have discovered that many mothers have a desire to work from home but needed guidance in how to do so.

As a Christian mother, I feel that my first priority is to God and then my family. My at-home work comes after that. I'm constantly re-evaluating my workload to make sure I am not neglecting my relationship with God, husband, or children. I firmly believe that a Christian mother's decision to work from home needs to take into account God, family, and calling.

This book attempts to address those issues, as well as provide a solid foundation for starting at-home employment. You will find the tools and information to help you decide if working from home is right for you, and you will discover how to be successful in your at-home work.

As Christian stay-at-home mothers, we can use our talents in a way that contributes to our families' income, fulfills our desires, and glorifies God.

1

So You Want to Work from Home

What is your calling beyond caring for your family and home?

Once upon a time, in a far away kingdom, there lived a woman who had many children. While her husband attended to important business matters, she lovingly took care of the house, servants, and children. By her every thought and action, she brought joy and laughter to her household.

She took pride in running her household smoothly and made sure that her family and servants had all that they needed. She carefully kept track of the household expenses so that they never ran short of funds.

In addition, this woman transacted business from home. For example, she purchased a building and then sold it to invest the profits into another business venture. She also sewed garments to sell to local merchants. In all of this, she did not neglect those *less fortunate, extending a helping hand to the poor and needy of her community.*

She rejoiced in her blessings and talked kindly to and of others. Her husband and children praised her. Her own works and actions caused her to be praised throughout the land.

Sound familiar? This paraphrase of Prov. 31:10-31 shows an extraordinary woman, one who, like you, wears many hats: wife, mother, nurse, cook, cleaner, accountant—and businesswoman, who runs successful ventures from her home. As this passage indicates, we stay-at-home mothers can fulfill our God-given responsibilities to care for our husbands, children, and home— all while running a home-based business or working from home.

Each of us has different situations in life, but God also has equipped us with different talents and temperaments to meet those challenges. As Christian women, we are called to do what God has best fitted us to do.

But what exactly are Christian mothers "best-fitted" to do? Being a stay-at-home mother is a full-time job in and of itself. (In chapter 4, we will look at how to evaluate your personal responsibilities in light of working from home.)

Today, in some evangelical circles, we as Christian women may believe that it is sinful to yearn to do anything outside of caring for our children and our routine household chores. But seeking fulfillment in things outside of home-related chores does not mean we are selfish, as long as we remember to examine our motives and make sure we are not seeking after our own pleasure to the detriment of our relationships with God, our husbands, and our children. The fact that we want to use our gifts and abilities can be a God-given desire to glorify Him through the talents He has given us.

There are many different seasons in our lives, and working from home could be one. As Solomon puts it, *There is a time for everything, a season for every activity under heaven.... What do people really get for all their hard work? I have thought about this in connection with the various kinds of work God has given people to do.* (Eccl. 3:1, 9-11)

"My husband and I feel that it is not 'un-Christian' for mothers to work outside the home, but since we are in a position where I can work part-time from home, or even choose not to work at all, we are taking advantage of that blessing," says Lori Boyd Schantz, who lives in Upper Darby, Pennsylvania, with her husband and one-year-old daughter.

A senior scientist with a Washington, D.C., based research organization, she says her decision to work from home stemmed from a desire to limit others' care of her daughter. "I want to raise my daughter in our home and with minimal outside childcare. My husband and I feel that I should stay home to teach, discipline, encourage, and provide a Christian role model for our daughter. Working at home allows me to do this and work at a job I love."

But before you decide whether as a Christian stay-at-home mother you should work from home, let's examine the calling of a Christian mother.

Your calling

As Christians, our calling is to glorify God. The Apostle Paul writes about this calling in his letter to the Ephesians:

How we praise God, the Father of our Lord Jesus Christ, who has blessed us with every spiritual blessing in the heavenly realms because we belong to Christ.

Long ago, even before he made the world, God loved us and chose us in Christ to be holy and without fault in his eyes. His unchanging plan has always been to adopt us into his own family by bringing us to himself through Jesus Christ. And this gave him great pleasure.

So we praise God for the wonderful kindness he has poured out on us because we belong to his dearly loved Son. (Eph. 1:3-6)

Our entire life as a person is a calling from God (1 Cor. 7 and 1 Pet. 2). This covers our daily work—what we do to earn money—and our family and friend relationships. It's important to remember that we need to seek to glorify God through every task or circumstance in our lives, even those not overtly spiritual in nature.

For example, we glorify God in mundane household chores, like washing dishes, scrubbing toilets, and cooking dinner, as well as in more spiritual activities, such as teaching our children about God, reading the Bible, praying for ourselves and others, and attending corporate worship at church. For wives and stay-at-home mothers, part of this calling to glorify God is to care for our husbands, children, and household as unto the Lord.

I believe Scripture teaches that God intends for the home to be the wife's domain. We should embrace that calling to be workers at home—caring for our husbands and children, and to keep a well-run and clean household. While not a popular view, it is a biblical one:

She carefully watches all that goes on in her household and does not have to bear the consequences of laziness. (Prov. 31:27)

This does not necessarily mean we have to do everything ourselves; at times, it may be prudent to have outside help with meals, cleaning, or childcare. For each family, this will look different, but we need to make sure we are paying attention to what God has called us to do in our homes.

Mothers should have a renewed sense of this calling to take care of our households, whether or not we work from home. We should cultivate this calling through relationships that encourage our work as a wife and mother, and through our own commitments to grow in that work. Once we fully embrace this calling as wives and mothers, then we can explore other ways we may be called to serve God with our lives.

"I knew that my calling beyond glorifying God was to my family," says stay-at-home mom and graphic designer Martha Leone, who lives in Springfield, Virginia, with her husband and three children. Martha carefully weighed her decision to work from home in light of that calling.

Answering your call

So, could a Christian mother's calling as a worker at home include work from home? I certainly think so. God created everyone different and gave us unique gifts, talents, and abilities. For some women those gifts and abilities may be best put to use outside the home, either in volunteer work for the church or community or in paid employment.

For others, their talents can enhance their family's life, such as developing creative activities for the children or decorating the house. Many women use their abilities in a combination of ways, both inside and outside the house.

Jesus illustrates this very idea in the parable of the talents: *To those who use well what they are given, even more will be given, and they will have an abundance. But from those who are unfaithful, even what little they have will be taken away.* (Matt. 25:29)

Many Christian women feel that they honor God by working—either from home or outside the home—because they are utilizing the gifts and abilities with which God has endowed them. A person's vocation is an integral part of his or her Christian calling.

Valerie Ottinger, who lives in Cumming, Georgia, with her husband, was a public school teacher when she and her husband married.

"I have always been very organized, but I'm a perfectionist who tends to focus on one thing at a time," she says. "This is one reason why I was so concerned about getting married and continuing my teaching job. I felt that I couldn't be a good wife and mother and a good teacher at the same time.

"From what I observed and from women I talked to about it, few succeed at both simultaneously. My poor husband was sadly neglected the first year of our marriage as I ran ragged, trying to keep up with the demands of teaching."

Through a change in circumstances relating to her husband's job, Valerie was able to quit teaching and found at-home work as a circulation manager for a Protestant denominational magazine based in the area.

"I didn't want to stop working altogether, and my husband knows I'd go crazy without some kind of job," she explains. "I'm humbled that God provided a job that met my ideal expectations and that allows me to work from home."

Check your motives

One way we as Christian women can discern our calling is through prayer. Prayerfully evaluate your motives, asking God to reveal any sin in your desire to work from home.

If you think working from home fits with your current "season of life," then perhaps you should talk with an older Christian woman about this possibility to help sort out your thoughts and feelings on the matter.

Similarly, teach the older women to live in a way that is appropriate for someone serving the Lord. These older women must train the younger women to love their husbands and their children, to live wisely and be pure, to take care of their homes, to do good, and to be submissive to their husbands. Then they will not bring shame on the word of God. (Titus 2:3-5)

Cultivate relationships with these godly women so that you can receive—and give—encouragement as you grow in your Christian walk and vocation.

Ask yourself tough questions that may reveal both positive and negative motives:

Why do I want to work from home? Is it to avoid feeling like a non-person? To find fulfillment outside my calling as a wife and mother? To become a more interesting person? To be of help to others through your work? To enhance my calling? To help my family's finances? To find an outlet for the talents God has given me? To garner more material possessions? To fund my own special projects or purchases? To usurp my husband of his God-given responsibility to provide for his family?

Consider Paul's admonishment in Colossians as you examine your heart:

Work hard and cheerfully at whatever you do, as though you were working for the Lord rather than for people. Remember that the Lord will give you an inheritance as your reward, and the Master you are serving is Christ. (Col. 3:23-24)

Right motives include being content with your present situation, being thankful to the Lord for your calling as a wife and mother, glorifying God in all things, and submitting to your husband as head of your household. Along each step of the journey toward working from home, follow the advice of Prov.16:3: *Commit your work to the LORD, and then your plans will succeed.* 🏠

Martha Leone
Graphic Designer

For Martha Leone, a mother of five-year-old twins and a six-year-old, the opportunity to work from her home in Springfield, Virginia, as a graphic designer came out of the blue. "I got a call from a former colleague who had started her own business. She wanted to know if, despite having three preschoolers at home, I was ready to start freelancing," she explains.

Before having children, Martha was an art director for a corporate communications design firm. "I knew that in my field, it's fairly easy to work from home. And I enjoyed what I did when I worked full time," says Martha. "So when my former co-worker created a situation that gave me creative graphic design work and the freedom to work on a by-project basis, I accepted."

From the beginning, Martha emphasized her desire to have flexibility to work around her family's schedules. In order to maintain that flexibility, she decided not to travel to face-to-face meetings with clients. She set strict guidelines for herself and communicated those to the people she worked with in order to manage expectations.

Before committing to working from home, Martha and her husband talked about the costs involved in setting up her home office. "We needed to determine the purchase price of computer and office equipment and to designate a work space for me within our house. We also considered taxes and what my fee structure should be based on the market rate for someone at my skill level," she says.

They also discussed how her working from home might change the family dynamics. "We already had begun to teach our kids the importance of cheerful service to one another and their individual contribution to our family. Our children took on more responsibility by performing age-appropriate chores, such as helping me prepare dinner," Martha explains.

The biggest change for Martha is how tight her daily schedule can become when she's working on a project. "It was important to set a weekly work schedule for myself that allowed set pockets of time for freelance. With schedule in hand, I can run to the park with the kids without fretting over a deadline. I'll make phone calls in the early afternoon while the kids are resting and do the actual creative work during those pre-determined hours, at night or early morning."

She likes the ebb and flow of a freelancer's schedule. Some weeks she's really busy and some weeks she doesn't have any projects. "When I was single, I worked long hours and was driven to succeed. Now, with a family to care for and enjoy, I still desire to do good work, but I will take on fewer projects in order to continue to fulfill my God-given calling as a wife and mother."

Overall, Martha is thankful for this opportunity to work from home. "God has enabled me to enjoy this type of work and has provided clients who support me as a mother and designer."

Valerie Ottinger
Circulation Manager

Although she doesn't have children yet, Valerie Ottinger is preparing for their arrival by working from home. "In my previous job as a public school teacher, I observed many of my non-Christian colleagues who had their babies and returned to the classroom six to eight weeks later," she says. "It was heart-wrenching to see, and I couldn't do that to our children. My husband and I had decided that when we had kids, I would quit my full-time job, but we couldn't live on his salary alone."

When her husband found another job, they relocated to Cumming, Georgia, near her husband's family, and Valerie began looking for suitable at-home employment. "Neither of us wanted a job that would take me away from our children, when they came along, for long periods of time. I had always thought that my ideal job would be flexible and allow me to use my English degree as I worked at home on a part-time basis."

Six months ago, she found a part-time job as a circulation manager with a Protestant denominational magazine with offices nearby. Working twenty hours a week, she handles subscriptions and customer service duties at home, with one day a week in the office.

Transitioning to at-home work has its share of challenges, she says. "If you're not self-disciplined or self-motivated, it's hard to schedule your own hours at home and follow them. My biggest challenge is simply getting started, although once I have started, it's actually hard to stop for lunch or give myself a deserved break."

She relies on advice and encouragement from the Flylady website (*www.flylady.net*), which provides tips on how to keep schedules and balance housework with other activities. "In the morning when it's time to 'go to work,' I let myself get distracted by my to-do list for the house, e.g., the laundry, cleaning, mending, gardening, and the myriad small tasks that comprise household work. It's easier for me to start my office work knowing the house is clean and de-cluttered, but the house will not always be in that condition. I need to set my hours and get in the habit of starting my office work anyway."

Distractions such as television, surfing the Internet, answering personal emails, focusing on housework instead of office work, and playing with the dog can be hard for her to ignore. "Another disadvantage is the lack of immediate accountability, meaning that no supervisor is at your house watching you as you're supposed to be working. Short breaks could stretch into hours. My moods can dictate whether I 'feel' like working," says Valerie.

But she loves the flexible schedule that allows her to get more housework done and set up the best time for exercise. "If I've been staring at the computer for an hour, and the dryer beeps, I can take a quick break while I go downstairs to fold the laundry and put it away (not to mention the exercise from using the stairs). When we have kids, I'll also be able to work around their schedules."

Lori Boyd Schantz
Senior Scientist

Lori Boyd Schantz segued from her job as senior scientist for a Washington, D.C.-area research organization into an at-home position even before having children. When she and her husband moved out of the Washington, D.C., area to Upper Darby, Pennsylvania, she began to work full time from home, conducting job analysis, creating multiple-choice and performance-based tests, data analysis, educational research and quality assurance, and training development. After the birth of their daughter a year ago, and with her husband's full support, she has transitioned easily to working from home without children to doing so with a child.

"My husband is fully supportive of my job, but he also routinely reminds me I can quit whenever I want to," she says. "I like my job and I wanted to continue my work through some interesting projects and see if it was possible to juggle or balance both worlds, all from home."

Since Lori already worked from home before having her daughter, she simply had to scale back to part-time to accommodate her daughter's schedule. She now logs in 20 hours a week doing the same job but with fewer clients. "I created a certain structure and discipline working from home two years before our daughter was born. This has helped as I structure my work time during her naps," says Lori.

As with many work-from-home moms, Lori admits that at-home work is not always easy. "People assume my work must not be stressful since I can do it from home, or that my schedule is entirely flexible. I find it hard to stop working, thinking I could send one more email or work on this report just a little more, such as after our daughter goes to bed. Sometimes when I have to be on the computer or phone, or just working when our daughter is awake, she wants to play with my keyboard or the phone, and it's hard to stay focused."

For Lori, the advantages to working from home are many. "I can use my training and skills to perform my work well, and I feel a sense of satisfaction in doing good work, earning some income, and maintaining relationships with colleagues."

Whitney Hopler
Freelance Writer and Editor

For nine years, Whitney Hopler has worked from her Fairfax, Virginia, home as a writer and editor for a variety of online and print publication clients. Depending on her assignments, Whitney spends between ten and thirty-five hours each week on her work.

"I thought and prayed about it a lot while I was expecting my first child, and God made it clear to both my husband and me that he wanted me to continue my writing ministry without resorting to daycare," she says. "We were confident that God would provide both the opportunities for me to work from home, and the time and energy for me to do so—and he has abundantly provided all of that over the years."

Now with two children ages nine and one, Whitney enjoys the focus her work gives her. "I think that if I wasn't working from home I would be prone to wasting time, like talking to friends too long on the phone or surfing the Internet to deal with boredom. My assignments give me creatively fulfilling tasks to look forward to each day, so I'm never bored. I'm motivated to be disciplined because often I can hardly wait to write," she says.

While she sometimes neglects housework to finish an article, that doesn't bother her family. "My husband and children are flexible about helping out more when I have a heavy workload." For Whitney, the keys to successfully planning a work-from-home schedule include making work a priority and being flexible about completing household tasks.

Sometimes, Whitney has a mother's helper to assist with entertaining her youngest while she's on a deadline. She enjoys taking time off whenever she needs to without having to ask a supervisor for permission. "I'm able to be available to my kids when they need and want me to be there for them, while still getting my work done."

She offers a few tips gleaned from her years as a freelance writer to at-home mothers who want to work from home. "Choose work that you genuinely enjoy and sense God's calling to pursue, rather than just trying to make some money. Take your work as seriously as you would any job you could do outside your home. Protect your work schedule by learning how to say 'no' to distractions and requests for your time and energy that may be good, but simply don't align with God's vision for your life and your core values. Simplify your lifestyle and let go of tasks that don't really matter, such as cooking every dinner from scratch and vacuuming your carpets every day.

"I think that far too many Christian moms lack the confidence they need to consider working from home, because, too often, church culture celebrates traditional stay-at-home moms but negatively judges moms who pursue careers from home," says Whitney.

"Moms who work from home can have a hard time finding other Christians who will encourage them to genuinely seek God's calling in this area and urge them to use their talents professionally while at home with their kids. I believe strongly that if God is calling a particular mom to work from home, she will become a better mother if she decides to do so. She'll inspire her kids because they'll see her contributing and growing in all the ways God intends."

Resources
Books

The Call: Finding and Fulfilling the Central Purpose of Your Life
by Os Guinness

The Callings: The Gospel in the World
by Paul Helm

The Christian's Daily Walk
by Henry Scudder

Live Your Calling: A Practical Guide to Finding and Fulfilling Your Mission in Life
by Kevin Brennfleck and Kay Marie Brennfleck

Family Matters

What is your family situation?

E very family is different, with a unique set of circumstances. Evaluating your responsibilities in light of your
husband, children, home, and other obligations should be
a top consideration when thinking about working from home.
(In chapter 4, we will explore your personal time and daily
schedule.)

Your husband

As a wife, your first responsibility after your relationship with
God should be your relationship with your husband. As wives,
we are called biblically to submit to our husbands:

*You wives will submit to your husbands as you do to the Lord.
For a husband is the head of his wife as Christ is the head of his
body, the church; he gave his life to be her Savior. As the church
submits to Christ, so you wives must submit to your husbands in
everything.* (Eph. 5:22-24)

One way this submission plays out in thinking about a home-based business is by making sure your work from home does not interfere with your relationship with, and care of, your husband.

Part of that care involves considering and talking about how his job may be impacted by your work from home. Think about and answer these questions: What is his work schedule? Does his job require long hours? Extensive travel? Does he need to work nights or weekends? Would he be available for any child-care if needed?

Talk frankly with your husband about how he views your responsibilities to him, to your children, to the home, and to others. As a stay-at-home mom, you already have a full-time job in the home. Be honest with each other—it's better to find out before starting to work from home what his expectations are, so you can help to alleviate any misunderstandings or resentments later as your daily activities change to accommodate working.

Discuss with your spouse these questions: Is a home-cooked meal expected every night? Can you complete some household chores less frequently, such as mopping or vacuuming once a week instead of twice? Will you be able to run errands during the weekdays or will they need to be done on the weekend or evenings? Does your husband mind if you work at night? Would he be willing to take on more household chores to free up some of your time to work?

"How do we make it work in a way that my husband feels honored?" asks Julie Divine, mother of a one-year-old daughter and an at-home communications consultant from Colorado Springs, Colorado. "I don't want my work to take priority over my husband and daughter. Together, my husband and I have to keep talking and praying about my work from home. Our marriage is definitely a team, and each of us needs to understand the other's work-related pressures."

Discussing these issues with your husband can guide both of you in deciding whether working from home would be feasible for you at this time. You may find that it would be best for you to revisit the idea at a later date.

Your kids

At different ages, children require different things from their mothers. Parents of infants and toddlers, for example, have to meet nearly all of their children's needs, but as children grow older, so does their ability to do things for themselves. Many mothers stay at home in order to be there for their children—but "there" can mean a host of things depending on the age of the child, his development, schooling options, and other considerations. An at-home job also might be the perfect way to transition to life without children when your kids go off to college or leave the home for jobs or marriage.

Here are some questions to consider as you think about caring for your children and working from home: How much time do you spend each day in direct care of your children, such as feeding, changing diapers, interacting, and playing? How much time do you spend taking them places, such as to classes, sports, playgroups, etc.? How much time do you have to yourself because of school, naps, or rest time? How well do your children play, read, or otherwise entertain themselves? Jot down how long all of these tasks and activities generally take—then you'll begin to see what your daily schedule might look like. Chapter 4 offers more insight into finding time to work from home.

"God has given me the incredible blessing and responsibility of being the mother of my two children," says attorney Laura Barbour in Jackson, Mississippi. "And I feel that the best way I can be a mom is to be home with them. At the same time, God has blessed me with a legal education that has enabled me to benefit my family financially without having to sacrifice time with my children."

When thinking about caring for your children while working from home, remember to focus on how you and your husband view child-rearing. Don't borrow others' expectations for what raising a child might look like in your home.

Sit down with your husband and write down or talk in-depth about your ideas on raising children. What are your values and how will they be passed on to your children? What are the current and future needs of each child? Will you homeschool your children? What are your views of extra-curricular activities? What kind of parents do you want to be?

If your children are older, you could ask their input after explaining how things might change if you added a work-from-home job to your day.

For example, you might have them ride the school bus instead of driving them each day in order to gain time in the mornings and afternoons. You might need to have them pare back the number of after-school activities in which they are involved because you need their help around the house more. (Chapter 11 will give tips on how to juggle family, work, and me-time.)

Your home

Keeping up with housework generally falls to stay-at-home moms. If you take on outside work, the amount of time you have to devote to the home's appearance might diminish significantly.

The entire family needs to be on board to help you in this endeavor, so see if your spouse would be willing to help out with shopping and cleaning tasks. If your kids are old enough, you could assign more household chores to them.

If your income allows, perhaps you need to outsource some of the cleaning or yard maintenance on a regular or special occasion basis (like getting the house ready for company or a deep spring cleaning). When my workload increased while writing this book, my husband stepped in to take over a few more weekly chores around the house.

Sometimes, you simply need to schedule certain household tasks in order to fit them into your weekly schedule. You may not be able to get to them every day. However, if clients regularly come to your home, you will need to make sure it is clean in order to make a good impression.

"As a piano teacher, I need to make sure my home is presentable and ready for students by a certain time every day," says Andrea Malcomson, a Helena, Montana, mother of three girls ages seven, three, and one.

The rest of your life

Working from home may affect other responsibilities you have, such as care of elderly parents, volunteer jobs, civic duties, and church-related activities. For example, I'm on the membership committee of our neighborhood swimming pool, for which I receive a discount on my annual dues.

My responsibilities include updating applications, keeping up with the pool's website, marketing the pool to potential members, answering emails about membership, and planning a membership open house. Since the pool opens Memorial Day weekend, my busiest time for pool-related activities is the spring; therefore, I generally scale back my freelance writing and editing assignments during that time frame in order to meet my pool obligations on the membership committee.

For some, you may need to allow time to disengage from volunteer work or to step back on involvement in church, civic, or other outside activities in order to devote those hours to starting a home-based business. However, don't be too hasty in dropping your involvements. Try divesting yourself of one activity at a time to see how that change reorders your schedule. You can always add the activities back into your agenda if you find time permits.

Whatever your family situation, a hard look at your obligations and an open and honest talk with your spouse is key to developing a healthy attitude toward the possibility of working from home.

Laura Barbour
Attorney

When Laura Barbour had her first child, she decided to put her legal career on hold to be a stay-at-home mom. By the time her daughter turned one, Laura saw she had more free time than expected. "When my daughter started taking longer naps in the afternoon, I realized that I could use that time to contribute to my family's income while doing something that I loved—legal research and writing," says Laura, who lives in Jackson, Mississippi, with her husband, four-year-old daughter and two-year-old son.

Laura squeezes in ten to fifteen hours of work a week during her children's nap and preschool time. "My husband has been very supportive," she says. "He is also an attorney, so we often review each other's work."

She misses the adult interaction and camaraderie of an office environment but considers the time spent with her children a fair trade. The hardest part of working from home is "meeting deadlines. I really have to plan ahead because I have a limited amount of time in the day to work," says Laura.

Julie Divine
Communications Consultant

Before having children, Julie Divine worked as a communications consultant, helping nonprofits with grant and brochure writing, and developing overall communications plans and strategies. She negotiated a part-time arrangement with her employer before the birth of her daughter, now a one-year-old.

"I work mostly from home," she says, adding that she goes into the office one or two days a week. "It started out as mostly from home; as she's gotten older, I need some uninterrupted time that's not at night but during business hours to make calls."

She spends about twenty-four hours a week at her job,

which she finds manageable. "Working from home is great, but I'm always looking for those chunks of time to do it."

For Julie, deciding to work from home sprang from a desire to be the primary caregiver of her child. "Working from home allows me to supplement our income and to continue pursuing my interests. One plus is that I do not have to take my daughter to childcare every day," says Julie, who lives in Colorado Springs, Colorado.

Her husband has been appreciative that she can use her skills and supplement their income. "He really tries to take the lead in helping around the house when I've got a deadline and need three hours of uninterrupted time," she says.

"Time is so precious, and I can't completely anticipate what my day will look like," she says of her at-home job. "I am constantly thinking, 'How productive can I be in thirty minutes of time?' or 'What three things can I get done during naptime?'"

Sometimes, though, work hangs over her head while she's spending time with her daughter. "The second she's down for a nap or playing quietly, I make a few work calls," says Julie. "I often feel like I'm in some stage of work-mode all the time. But I also feel a sense of freedom not having to work full time. We're able to squeeze in fun things every day."

While some days she struggles to give work and her daughter the attention they need, she appreciates the fact that she can work from home. "When things go smoothly, I'm re-energized and able to give my daughter a happy, focused mommy," she says. "I have a great situation with an employer that allows flexibility. I would encourage other moms just to see what the options are in relation to working from home."

Andrea Malcomson
Piano Teacher

Andrea Malcomson taught music in public schools before having her first daughter seven years ago. "I wanted to stay home with my first baby and we needed the additional income, so I began giving piano lessons in my home," she says. Now with three girls ages seven, three, and one, Andrea spends six hours a week teaching piano, in addition to homeschooling.

"I love being my own boss, setting my own schedule and rate of pay," says the Helena, Montana-based Andrea. Her husband is very supportive and helps with the homeschooling.

"My schedule works well for my kids' nap times and students' availability," she says. "However, I often have to organize dinner ahead of time to fit my work schedule."

One drawback of self-employment for Andrea is that it doesn't provide benefits. "Sometimes, it is awkward when I have to remind student's parents to pay their monthly tuition," she further admits.

But she's very glad to be able to contribute financially to the family and stay at home. "I want to encourage other mothers out there that working from home is possible," says Andrea. "It does take a lot of hard work, but it is worth it for the sake of the kids."

Holly Dutton
Church Worship Director

Two years ago, Holly Dutton transformed her love of music into an unusual at-home job: that of a worship director at her church. "I felt like I needed to work," she says. "Some of that was a financial need, but most of it was feeling called to do what I do."

She works about thirty hours a week, and most of the work is done from her Norfolk, Virginia, home. "On the weekend, I have stuff that I do at the church, but during the week from home, I write the charts for musicians, arrange the schedule, and take care of making other plans for the worship team," she explains.

While her three-year-old son is in preschool three mornings a week, she meets with musicians for discipleship and to talk about the week's activities. "I really love music and felt like it was a gift that God wants me to use," she says. "Being a worship director seemed like a logical fit for me."

Sometimes, she feels guilty about not giving enough time and attention to her son. "I have experienced an external and self-imposed pressure to limit my activities to raising our son and keeping our home," says Holly. "And I have certainly felt guilty about not doing that. However, I also was raised by a single mother who had to work, and because of that, I became a very independent person. Over time, I felt like I was a square peg cramming myself into a round hole. Now I believe that God uses these circumstances to allow us to serve in different ways."

Her husband is very glad she can contribute to the household income. "He appreciates that I have an outlet for my creativity, and a way to use my skills and gifts in a way that is useful," says Holly. "I know there have been times it has been frustrating for him because I am so tired—sometimes from working and being a mother—that not everything gets done around the house, or things fall short as far as disciplining our son."

Staying focused can be a challenge for Holly, as "there's always some pile of laundry that needs to be done, and so many distractions and ways I can put off doing what needs to be done. But I think that I would find distractions if I was in the workplace, too. This is the work that I love and I feel invested in. Sometimes I must compromise, but in the end, everything gets done."

She struggles to give one hundred percent at any given moment to either motherhood or musicianship. "Many times my projects don't come off the way I want them to because I don't have enough energy to invest in them," she explains. "However, all in all, the pros outweigh the cons for our family. There's a lot of flexibility in at-home work. I make my own schedule, work at my own pace, and have so much more control over what I do and how it is done."

She is heartened to hear that her work is meaningful. "If God doesn't mean for it to be, then he will close that door."

Working from home gives her much more freedom than previous nine to five jobs, she says. "Working from home allows me to do more with the gifts I have in a creative way. This really enriches our son's life. He gets to see his mommy at work and understands that even mommies have careers, whether in the workplace or at home."

Resources
Books

The Excellent Wife: A Biblical Perspective
by Martha Peace

What's a Smart Woman Like You Doing At Home?
by Linda Burton, Janet Dittmer, and Cheri Loveless

Online

Family and Home Network
P.O. Box 545
Merrifield, VA 22116
703-352-1072
www.familyandhome.org
fahn@familyandhome.org
Family and Home Network supports the needs of full-time mothers.

MOPS International, Inc.
2370 South Trenton Way
Denver, CO 80231-3822
303-733-5353
800-929-1287
www.mops.org
info@mops.org
Mothers of Preschoolers helps all kinds of moms with infants through kindergarten-age children.

3

Can You Afford This?

Your financial situation

Before you commit to a home-based business, you need to evaluate your financial picture during the decision-making process. You already may know you need additional income to make ends meet, but getting a clear picture of your finances beforehand will help you pick the right at-home job.

Because some home-based businesses require start-up cash for equipment, office supplies, and product, knowing your personal financial situation before getting started can provide you with a better understanding of where those funds may be found. (Chapter 8 covers the specifics on funding for a start-up business.)

Since there are many good books and websites out there that provide in-depth coverage for getting your financial house in order, this chapter only will hit the highlights of finding your net worth and working within a spending plan. (See the resource list at the end of the chapter for specific titles and websites for more information.)

Your net worth

Your first step in focusing on your financial picture is to figure out your net worth. A net worth statement provides a snapshot of your financial situation by showing how much you would have if everything you own was liquidated to cash and used to pay off all your debts.

To find out your net worth, simply make a list of all your assets. Included in this list would be assets that are not fully paid off, such as your house or cars. You will have two separate lists, one for appreciating assets, such as your home and the cash in your savings accounts; and depreciating assets, such as your personal property and vehicles.

Next, assign a reasonable value to each item. For assistance, check your real estate assessment statement you receive for tax purposes to get a good idea of your home's value, or you can look in your local paper to see the recent sale prices of comparable houses in your neighborhood.

For automobiles, several online sites, such as Kelley Blue Book (*www.kbb.com*) or Edmunds (*www.edmunds.com*), offer free assessments. Check your homeowner's policy or personal property insurance to add any other assets, such as personal property, musical instruments, jewelry, artwork, or antiques that you might have separately insured. Also add accounts where your money might be parked, such as 401(k) funds, IRA accounts, college-savings accounts, savings accounts, CDs, money-market accounts, checking accounts, investments or stock portfolios, and credit-union accounts.

Then you are ready to list your debts, or liabilities. This includes what you owe on your mortgage, car, credit cards, home-equity loans, student loans, and any other debts or personal loans you may have.

Add up your assets and your liabilities separately; then subtract your liabilities from your assets. That number, negative or positive, is your net worth. Calculating your net worth on an annual basis gives you a good overall picture of how your financial situation fluctuates from year to year. One advantage to figuring your net worth is that you'll have a list of all your debts, which you may want to pay off using some of the income from your home-based business. You may also find available cash to fund your at-home work.

Jane and John Doe's Net Worth Statement		
ASSETS-APPRECIATING		
Cash in Checking Account	$2,336.85	
Cash in Savings Account	$7,350.00	
John's 401(k) Retirement	$30,940.03	
Jane's IRA Account	$16,969.05	
House	$275,000.00	
John Jr.'s College Savings	$5,000.00	
Janey's College Savings	$4,000.00	
Total Appreciating Assets		$341,595.93
ASSETS-DEPRECIATING		
Personal Property	$10,000.00	
Jewelry	$4,000.00	
Piano	$7,000.00	
2004 Toyota Sienna LE	$18,520.00	
2003 Honda Civic DX Sedan	$10,105.00	
Total Depreciating Assets		+ $49,625.00
TOTAL ASSETS		$391,220.93
LIABILITIES		
Home Mortgage	$185,000.00	
Car Loan, Sienna	$10,295.00	
Credit Card Debt	$2,342.00	
TOTAL LIABILITIES		- $197,637.00
NET WORTH		$193,583.93

A monthly snapshot

After calculating your net worth, you need to know what you spend each month. This will help you determine if there are any spending areas from which you can "borrow" to fund your home-based business until you are making a profit.

Start by keeping a daily journal of your expenses, writing down where every penny goes. Combine those daily accounts into a weekly and, finally, a monthly list. Then add up all your monthly income, including salary, wages, interest or dividends, alimony, child-support payments, and so on. Use pretax figures, as you might find you'll want to adjust your withholding. As with the net worth, subtract your monthly income from your monthly expenses. This is an extremely simplified version of a budget, or spending plan.

Because your at-home work might not bring in a dependable paycheck, at least at first, you should make sure your monthly expenses are covered by your husband's salary. For instance, my freelance writing clients take anywhere from ten days to up to two months to pay invoices, so I have learned not to spend the money before I have the check in hand. If your at-home work does bring in regular paychecks, then you can adjust your spending plan accordingly.

Use the information on your spending plan to ferret out areas where you can trim spending and free up cash for start-up costs for your business. Even jobs that do not require product or supplies for product will cost you something.

You may need general office supplies, such as file folders, pens, paper, ink cartridges for your printer or fax machine, stapler, hole puncher, or sticky notes; computer equipment or software upgrades; a faster Internet connection if you need constant access to the Web; a separate phone or fax line; cell phone; business cards; and mailing supplies and postage. You may be able to write off some or all of these at tax time, but consult a tax adviser for specifics. (Chapter 9 offers more information on tax issues for home-based businesses.)

"My husband and I started thinking about our options when I got pregnant," says Lisa Harmon, an office manager for a real estate appraisal firm in Raleigh, North Carolina. "We both really wanted for me to be able to stay home, but as we looked at our budget, it was impossible to take out my income. After much prayer and thought, I went to my boss and presented a carefully laid out plan for how I could work from home after the baby was born and I took a maternity leave."

Sometimes you can look at what you already have in the way of equipment or supplies and find a home-based business idea there. For example, when Dixie Moore's four children were young, she needed to supplement the family income, but wanted to stay home to rear her children. "My husband and I were committed to my being at home to create a place that was functioning and nurturing for our family, other children, and friends," says Dixie, who lives on a farm in Bainbridge Island, Washington. "We had sheep, I knew how to knit, and I liked children, so I started teaching children to knit. It all came together as a creative way to work at home, and I only had to work for a few hours a week."

Figure out your income

While reviewing your monthly spending plan, consider how your income from your at-home work could be allocated. Just remember that, as Suzanne Venker, author of *7 Myths of Working Mothers*, points out, "What many women still haven't figured out is that less is more. A second income may provide their families with more things, yes, but this doesn't necessarily make the family better off."[15] Most at-home businesses start slowly and take time to build up a client or customer base that would bring in a good income. Keeping your monetary expectations conservative can assist in planning where your income will go.

If you are moving from working outside the home to an at-home job, your earnings already may be designated for certain bills or expenses. If you do not need your earnings for monthly expenses, carefully consider what your money will fund. If you don't have a specific place for the money to go, you might find that it "magically" seems to vanish.

For example, we have used money from my freelance writing

to pay for master's degrees for both my husband and me; to go on a cruise; to purchase furniture; and to pay for car and computer repairs. We also give ten percent to charity, ten percent to savings, and ten percent to my IRA account. We also put money aside to pay quarterly federal and state taxes. In addition, my husband also has a side job that we use to fund our three young children's college-savings accounts.

Ideas for where you can allocate your at-home work money could include private schooling, college funds or tuition, vacations, home improvements, monthly bills, car purchase or repairs, a home addition, home purchase or mortgage prepayment, giving to charity or church, helping out family members, getting out of debt, federal or state taxes relating to your business, and putting money back into your business for product, supplies, equipment repairs, or marketing and promotion.

"My husband and I know it would be extremely difficult for us to live on his salary alone," says Rebekah Matt, a copywriter who lives in St. Louis, Missouri, with her husband and four children ranging in ages from seven months to ten years. "I was still in contact with my old co-workers at the publishing house where I used to work. When I found out that they had experienced layoffs and were looking for freelance writers, I felt that it was an opportunity that had fallen into my lap, and I shouldn't pass it up. Even though I hadn't been actively looking for a paying position, I truly believe that God put this job in my path and has used it to help provide for our family for many years now."

Getting a clear view of your financial picture before starting a home-based business or job can be beneficial to your decision-making process. Knowing how much money you currently live on and what your monthly expenditures are can help you decide how to allocate your home-based business income in a way that will best meet your family's needs. 🏠

Lisa Harmon
Office Manager

Lisa Harmon turned her job as an office manager for a real-estate appraisal firm in Raleigh, North Carolina, into an at-home job when she became pregnant. Because her salary was needed in the family spending plan, she went to her boss with a plan for working from home. She started working from home after a short maternity leave and the birth of her daughter, now six months old.

"I was able to figure out how I could do almost everything from home. My company hired someone to be in the office a few hours in the morning to answer phones. I still do everything else, but from home instead of going into the office," she says. She does go into the office once a week while her mother watches her daughter. From home, she does all of the accounting, marketing, emailing, phone calling, organizing, and more. "I just had to do some research and figure out how to access everything I needed from home," says Lisa. She spends five hours a week in the office, and two to four hours a day working at home the other four days.

At first, she was concerned that she would be too busy to enjoy time with her daughter, but she was able to let go of her responsibility as organizer of the children's ministry at her church to free up more time. Her husband really wanted her to be able to stay home with their child, so he helped her set up an office at home and has continued to be supportive as new things pop up and she needs help. "He is thrilled that I can be home with our daughter and still bring in some income," she says.

Working from home has changed her daily schedule immensely, she says. "I used to have a set routine of going into the office, running errands, and coming home. Now, I have to plan my day based on my daughter's schedule and to figure out how to accomplish both work and home responsibilities. Combining those two is very hard some days."

When her infant daughter is fussy and Lisa needs to spend more time with her instead of getting work done, it can be challenging. And some days she doesn't get to leave the house because of work deadlines, which can be a disadvantage to at-home jobs. However, the pros outweigh the cons, says Lisa. She gets to spend more time with her daughter as her daughter develops physically and mentally, and she can fit her own schedule around her daughter's.

Rebekah Matt
Copywriter

"My number-one problem to overcome has been resentment that I have to work. It took me about eight years to work through this and come to a place of peace," says Rebekah Matt, a copywriter who lives in St. Louis, Missouri, with her husband and four children ages ten, eight, five and seven months.

"In some Christian circles, the wife is not supposed to work; the husband is supposed to provide, and, according to these Christians, be the only provider. Hearing this produces a lot of guilt and resentment among working Christian moms. Even though we may need to work to help support our families, and our husbands are supportive and in agreement with it, we feel 'unbiblical' or that something is defective about our husbands since we are in this situation. I don't believe that all Christian women should work, but I do think that they certainly can if circumstances call for it, and the husband and wife believe it's best," she says.

For Rebekah, her experience as a copywriter with a publishing house before she had children transferred easily to at-home work. The company she worked for needed freelance writers and she was able to fill that gap. For the past ten years, she has written direct marketing or advertising copy for health sciences publishers that sell professional references to doctors, nurses, veterinarians, dentists, and allied health professionals. She spends five to fifteen or more hours per week, depending on the workload and time of year, as some months have more mailings than others.

"My husband started seminary four years after I began working from home, and with taking classes part-time, it took him five and a half years to graduate," she says. "Those were difficult years for our family, but during that time, God provided for us in so many ways, and my work-at-home job was a great blessing to us. My husband continues to be supportive of my job. We would both like a situation where I didn't have to earn an income, but since that's not the case, we are making the best of it and working together to make it work for all of us."

Since her workload fluctuates from week to week, Rebekah says she needs to keep things in perspective and to not over-commit herself to church or homeschooling activities. "I can tell that when I'm busy, I'm more stressed," she says. "I need to be prepared to give up my evenings to work, and to share the computer with my husband if he has freelance work to do, too. Sometimes we trade off computer time, depending on who has the tighter deadline to meet."

She says one of the challenges that she faces working from home is having an infant in the house. "I was at a great point with the children being older and able to occupy themselves for periods of time during the day without me being right there with them—and then we had number four!," says Rebekah. "But the older children are a huge help, so I feel that the really hard times are behind me—the years when there were preschoolers, toddlers, and/or infants, but no older children. However, finding uninterrupted time is a challenge. I've trained myself to do quite a bit in tiny increments of time. I also have babysitters who come for three-hour stretches twice a month; when my children were younger, it was once a week. This is a big help and well worth the money spent."

Rebekah says she loves working from home. "I don't believe I could ever work in an office again—I'm spoiled!" She can accept or reject work depending on their finances, time, and family situation. She sets her own hours, working early in the morning or late at night in her pajamas. Her children also are with her while she works. "I wrote and corrected copy by hand while holding my sleeping newborn last summer," she says. There are also no office politics, gossip, endless meetings, non-productive chat time, annoying co-workers, dress codes, commute time, rush-hour traffic, dry cleaning bills, early alarm clocks, or worries about daycare—and she can take a break when it's a gorgeous day outside.

"I feel blessed to have a job that I can do from home," she says. "Thank goodness for the Internet and email, as it has made jobs like mine possible."

She encourages other moms who work from home to not compare themselves to other mothers who don't work. "For several years, I was surrounded by women with young children who didn't work. I compared myself to them and had little pity parties for poor me. I realize now that my work has been a gift from God and I appreciate it, rather than resent it."

Rebekah also reminds work-at-home mothers to suppress the desire to explain to others why they are working. "Telling people that you work in order to pay for basic living expenses is a very subtle slam against our husbands. We might as well say, 'My husband isn't able to provide for our family, so I have to help.' That's bad for our marriages, bad for ourselves, and bad for all working Christian women. The decision to work is between you and your husband and God—that's it."

Christian mothers who work from home need to stay in prayer over their jobs, says Rebekah. "Ask God to bless you and others through your work—not only your family, but others in your church and also people that you work with, both Christian and non-Christian. Thank God for providing this means of income for your family. Because many jobs can't be done from home, thank God for giving you the talents and abilities necessary for a work-at-home job.

"It took me many years to realize that my job was God's gift to me and to our family," she says. "Once I recognized that, I began to think of my work in an entirely different way. If I truly had a choice, I suppose I'd probably stop working—after all, I have four young children and I homeschool, so I could use the extra time! But while I am working, I try to keep a positive and, most importantly, a grateful attitude."

Dixie Moore
Children's Knitting Teacher

"I have tried to follow the example of the Proverbs 31 woman though the years," says Dixie Moore. "I see her as being a home manager, not necessarily doing all the work, but working smart. She chooses her endeavors wisely and provides work for others as well as herself to bring in income." Dixie, who lives on Bainbridge Island, Washington, with her husband and youngest child, started her knitting business fifteen years ago when her four children were small.

"For the Proverbs 31 woman, work and family seem very integrated. For her it's not a question of 'Should I work at home?' but rather 'What will be my work?' Work with the season you're in; don't run to live in another season that your family is not in," Dixie says.

With a master's degree in clinical counseling, her career might have taken a different path, but she and her husband wanted her to be home to raise their children, now ranging in ages from twenty-five to fourteen. They were raising sheep, and that, combined with her ability to knit, brought her to start her business.

"I teach small classes of children the basics of knitting," says Dixie. "My classes meet in a small studio on our property, where we knit, listen to music, read books, and chat. During the summers, I run about five fiber art day camps out of my studio, three hours a day. I hire fiber artists to come and explain their craft, and we play games, read books, knit, and generally have a good time. I currently teach classes through the local parks and recreation department at my studio and one class at a local elementary public school. Previous to that, I worked through a local yarn store as their children's instructor."

Dixie spends about three hours per week teaching and one to two hours a week preparing for the camps and making "surprise balls," which are made by winding up yarn into balls and hiding seven small toys inside that fall out as the young knitter knits. "The surprise balls started out as a side business, and have been a nice way to earn more money and encourage my knitters to knit more," she says.

Combining her students' tuition, Dixie averages between $40 and $50 an hour. "My husband has always been supportive of this job and regularly reminds me of what a good job it is, not only because it enriches children's lives, but also because I work so few hours for the amount of money I make," she says.

For Dixie, keeping work in its proper place helps to alleviate stresses that can come with working from home. "My first work is my family and home life," she says. "I am the manager of my home and time, so I don't let work manage me. I schedule my classes for the same day of the week, so I am only working a few hours on one day. For the most part, when I make my quarterly schedule, I schedule in margins for illness, mental health breaks, and family schedules. Consequently, I never resent my work."

She says she felt more challenged when her children were younger, but even so, she doesn't see any real disadvantages to working from home—only many advantages. "I am my own boss, and I am doing what I enjoy. I have a natural interest in knitting anyway, and I can build my own knowledge and skills as well. I am here for my family, and they admire my business rather than resent it. They have been able to work in my business, making wooden knitting needles, surprise balls, and assisting me in classes. This way, my business has provided income for them as well, as I paid my children to help me out."

The benefits of working at home for the Christian mom extend both within the family and beyond, according to Dixie. "You can influence many for good because of the freedom you have to make wise choices in how you will affect your family and sphere of contacts," she says. "To work at home, you can be creative, which has a ripple effect on your entire life. You can teach your children to be entrepreneurs, creative in their own right and blend that with serving people. Make what you do be a blessing to others; your clients, your family, yourself."

However, she cautions, if working from home is not working out for you or your family, you should stop. "It's not worth damaging your family, working all the time. Your place in the family is not to have everyone serve and honor you because you do such important work, but you are to serve and honor them first.

"I'm finding that when a woman commits herself to creating some good in her community through her work, she builds a reputation," explains Dixie. "In recent years, I've started to see some of my former knitters graduate from college and tell me they are still knitting. I have become aware of the number of lives that I have touched though the simple act of teaching one child at a time to knit."

Kathie Steinberg
Medical Transcriptionist

Kathie Steinberg used her background as a medical records supervisor at a residential treatment facility for troubled children as a stepping stone to her current at-home employment as a medical transcriptionist. "I had experience in transcription and the Lord brought this opportunity to me after I had started to pray two years ago about wanting to be home with my children," she says.

Now this South Bend, Indiana, mother of four children, ages seven, five, three, and one, works about twenty-five hours a week transcribing reports for several hospitals. Her husband really likes her being at home with the children, she says. "He has been one hundred percent behind the whole thing."

Since she started working from home, her children have adjusted to her new schedule. "At first, the three older ones didn't like it because they didn't see their friends at the babysitter's. Also, our babysitter was much more permissive than I was, so that was an adjustment, too. Now, everyone is fine with me working at home, especially since the middle two are in preschool."

Kathie has found that her daily schedule has changed from working outside the home—but not in the obvious way. "I don't have much time for myself at all between work, kids, housework, and errands. It seems weird, but I had a lot more time for me when I worked outside of the home," she says.

Most weeks, she needs to work at least five hours a day which can be difficult given that she has to make at least three trips a day to school to take children or pick them up. "Now there's not as much time to get things done, not much time for myself, and interruptions in my work," she says. "You adjust, though. Just like with anything else, you have good days and bad days. I hated my at-home job for at least the first six months because I didn't realize how time consuming it would be, especially at first because I didn't type as fast as I thought I could. Plus, it was hard to get used to the routine. Things did get better, though, and the Lord showed me a lot of grace."

While Kathie found the adjustment to work at home to be hard, she finds it worth it. "I don't ever want to work outside of the home again, even when my kids are not at home," she says.

Resources
Books

7 Myths of Working Mothers
by Suzanne Venker

The Family Financial Workbook: A Family Budgeting Guide
by Larry Burkett

Live Your Life For Half The Price
by Mary Hunt

The Christian's Guide to Money Matters for Women
by Mary Lynne McDonald

Online

Crown Financial Ministries
P.O. Box 100
Gainesville, GA 30503-0100
800.722.1976
www.crown.org
Provides financial information relating to families and businesses.

Debt-Proof Living
P.O. Box 2076
Paramount, CA 90723
800-550-3502
www.debtproofliving.com
Provides financial information relating to living within your means.

4

Do You Have
What it Takes?

Your personal situation

Whaat kind of person are you? Do you have what it takes to work at home or run a home-based business? As discussed in the previous chapters, if you have discerned that your calling as a wife and mother could expand to include working at home, if your family situation allows you to do so at this time, and if your financial picture would support an at-home business, then the next step is to see if you personally could work at home.

All about you

You may desire to work from home, but taking a closer look at the way you run your home and care for your children may reveal hidden depths or concerns that could affect you if you take on an additional responsibility. The following questions should help clarify how you view work and its inherent responsibilities.

Household issues

- *How much time do you spend on housework and meal preparation?*

- *On running errands?*

- *Is there quiet space in your home for an office or work place?*

Children issues

- *How much time do your children need from you each day? (This is especially critical if your children are not in school.)*

- *How independent are your children?*

- *Do you have childcare options available if needed?*

Personality issues

- *Are you frazzled at the end of a typical day?*

- *Are you a procrastinator?*

- *Can you meet deadlines?*

- *Do you handle pressure well?*

- *How do you handle interruptions or unexpected happenings?*

- *Do your days need a lot of structure?*

- *Are you more at ease with an open schedule?*

- *Can you motivate yourself to complete tasks?*

- *Do you need more direction or input from others to work well?*

- *How did you view working before marriage or children?*

- *Did you enjoy the office environment?*

Spiritual issues

- *Do you feel you have a genuine desire to use your God-given skills to benefit your family, community, and yourself?*

- *Do you feel that by working you are fulfilling your calling in Christ?*

"Sometimes, women do not understand the work world and how it functions," says Jennifer Smithfield, a Nashville, Tennessee-based mid-level manager for a group of research analysts. "You need to treat your at-home job as a job and operate the same way as you would in an office in order to fulfill your obligations to your employer or clients."

By taking the time to think through the answers to these and similar questions, you can get a fairly accurate picture of how you would manage the potential stresses and commitments that go with an at-home job.

All by myself

If you're a single mother, you may face different considerations when exploring at-home work. In addition to the questions in the section above, you might want to think about how you would connect with other adults in face-to-face work settings; how you would manage being home with your children all day and night, if childcare is not an option; how you would deal with the hours spent working and caring for your children; and how you would schedule time for yourself.

"A lot of times, I feel stretched," says single parent Betsy Hart, a Chicago-based newspaper columnist and radio show host. "I don't have a parent to help out with the children or who can put the kids to bed if I have a deadline and need to work. Sometimes, I'm exhausted, but that's just part of the deal."

"We are so isolated from other adults," adds single mom Rebecca Jean Rivera, who provides childcare in her home for two children in addition to her two boys in Atlantic Highlands, New Jersey. "I get absolutely no break from kids. This is my only source of income, so if I don't work, I don't get paid."

"If I had a young child, I couldn't do my job from home without daycare, as those are the rules my employer has established," says Denise Latimer, an inpatient coder for a larger hospital in Crystal, Minnesota, and single mother of two sons ages twenty-one and twelve. "I think people have thoughts that working from home is so much better than working in an office. It is still working. For me, it's less stressful but still a full-time job."

Time marches on

Home-based businesses or jobs take time, a precious commodity in anyone's life. Usually, you will have to devote more than a few hours a week to make your business succeed, and when you're trying to establish your at-home work, you may need to dedicate more hours to your business. In order to do a good job, you must be willing to sacrifice some of the things you spend time on now. Before you start your home-based business or take on an at-home job, think about the following questions.

Will you be able to cut back on some of the activities you enjoy doing to devote those hours to your business? Can you extract yourself from volunteer or church commitments at least while you're getting settled into your at-home work? Do you really want to sacrifice play group or soccer practice for conference calls? If you have preschool age children, are you ready to consider childcare options if necessary? If not, will you really have time to fit work into your daily schedule of caring for young children?

"I thought having a baby would just mean I would have to work while he was sleeping," says Lenore Ealy, who does consulting work for philanthropic organizations out of her home in Carmel, Indiana. "However, it didn't quite work out that way and I ended up working in the middle of the night when my son was little."

To see exactly how much time you could conceivably give to a job, keep a time journal for at least a week. Each day, from the moment you open your eyes until you close them at night, write down your activities in fifteen minute increments. Try to be as accurate as possible. You will be amazed at how quickly time flies—tasks you thought took only a few minutes can really take much longer.

Suzy Q. is a stay-at-home mother with two children, ages two and four. Take a look at a typical day in her life.

Suzy Q's Tuesday Time Journal

7:30 a.m.	Get up, make bed, get children up, make breakfast
8:00 a.m.	Eat breakfast, read the newspaper
8:30 a.m.	Help children get dressed
8:45 a.m.	Family devotions
9:00 a.m.	Wash breakfast dishes
9:15 a.m.	Shower and dress
9:45 a.m.	Sort laundry, start first load
10:15 a.m.	Check email, make phone calls
10:45 a.m.	Put first load of laundry into dryer, start second load
11:00 a.m.	Run errand
11:45 a.m.	Fix children's lunch
12:15 p.m.	Fix and eat own lunch
12:30 p.m.	Wash lunch dishes
12:45 p.m.	Finger puppet show for children
1:00 p.m.	Take children outside for a walk
1:30 p.m.	Fold and put away first load of laundry, put second load in dryer, start final load
2:00 p.m.	Get children down for rest/nap time
2:15 p.m.	Work on volunteer project for local historical society
3:00 p.m.	Fold and put away second load of laundry, put final load in dryer
3:15 p.m.	Finish working on volunteer project
4:00 p.m.	Fix snacks for kids

4:30 p.m.	Fold and put away final load of laundry
4:45 p.m.	Play with children
5:00 p.m.	Dinner preparation
5:30 p.m.	Husband home, talk about day
6:00 p.m.	Dinner
6:30 p.m.	Wash dinner dishes
7:00 p.m.	Bedtime preparation for children
7:30 p.m.	Bedtime for children
8:00 p.m.	Watch television and relax
10:00 p.m.	Get ready for bed
10:30 p.m.	Bedtime

Once you have a week's worth of time charted, examine it to see where you might have "time wasters," those chunks of time that don't really accomplish much at all. For me, time wasters include spending too much time reading the morning newspaper, taking long showers, constantly checking email, surfing the Web, watching television, and indulging in the occasional afternoon nap. These things in and of themselves are not bad, but they can gobble up time quickly. Sometimes I find myself falling behind in my household chores or freelance writing assignments wondering where the time went.

You'll probably spot pockets of time you could dedicate to working from home. If you are looking for full-time, at-home work, you need to either find a job or business where you can work odd hours or restructure your day to accomplish your job during the normal business hours of nine to five.

To free up more time, you might need to get up earlier, go to bed later (don't neglect your sleep, though!), schedule errands differently, stop watching television or DVDs, or curtail the time you spend in chat rooms or online in general.

However, be careful that you do not neglect your husband. And do not shut yourself off completely from your friends and family, or you will burn yourself out. In chapter 11 we'll look at specific ways to handle work, family, and me-time. 🏠

Lenore Ealy, Ph.D.
Philanthropy Consultant

"I'm a little more entrepreneurial-minded and found that working for an organization was a little bit constraining," says Lenore Ealy, who works as a consultant for philanthropic organizations from her home in Carmel, Indiana. Before working from home, she worked for public policy organizations as director for educational programs. Before her son, now seven, was born, she picked up freelance work writing grants and segued that work into consulting in the area of philanthropy and nonprofit management nine years ago.

"I work with nonprofit organizations writing grants, matching them up with funding, and helping with program development," she says. These days, she logs more than forty hours per week at her job, which now includes editing a journal on philanthropy.

"Before I had my son, it was a good, convenient way to work," she says. "Since I've had a child, I didn't want to go into a full-time office work environment." Because her job requires her to work at least forty hours a week, she arranged for a part-time nanny to help out with childcare when her son was little.

It is challenging to be one's own boss, Lenore admits. The networking required to generate clients is sometimes hard to come by. "You don't get out as much, so you rely very much on word-of-mouth referral," she explains. Although she is thankful for email and phones, which connect her to her clients, she misses having office support for her computer. And the social aspects of working in an office are not in place with a work-at-home job. "I miss getting coffee with an office buddy," she says.

Lenore has discovered that working at home can sometimes be quite as time-consuming and stressful as working in an office. "When I'm at home working, my days are very full, and I can't socialize and spend time with people who are friends," she says. She travels quite a bit for her job and so does her husband, which makes arranging their schedules quite difficult at times. "His calendar takes priority, but he's very supportive of my job," says Lenore.

Knowing when to quit working is sometimes hard for her. "If I'm in a middle of a project, I want to run back and finish it. It's hard to know how to separate family time and work time, and I have to discipline myself." To help stay disciplined, Lenore sets boundaries for herself. For example, she has made a personal rule that she will not check her email between three in the afternoon and eight in the evening in order to spend time with her son after school and to make dinner.

But she loves the schedule flexibility of a work-at-home job— especially the fact that when her son is sick or has snow days, she doesn't have to take off from work to be with him. "I can adjust to whatever the needs are," says Lenore. That flexibility also allows her to do a lot of volunteer work for her church.

Betsy Hart
Newspaper Columnist and Radio Show Host

For Betsy Hart, her primary motivating factor for working out of her home was having a flexible schedule in order to be available for her four children, ages thirteen, ten, eight, and five. "I need that flexibility, and with computers and the Internet, it's reasonable to work from home," she says.

Betsy writes her weekly newspaper column and preps for her weekly live radio show at home. Working from home also allows her to explore different avenues of income, depending on the flow of her work. For example, she wrote a book (*It Takes a Parent*) that led to her current radio show.

Her background as director of lectures and seminars for a conservative think tank, which she left after having her first child, has been a springboard to speaking engagements, too. She works about twenty hours a week at home, in addition to spending time at a Chicago studio doing her radio show once a week.

"My biggest challenge is to stop working," says Betsy. "We live in a twenty-four/seven society that enables me to send emails at two in the morning. Sometimes I have to be really disciplined to either say no to my kids or no to my computer. My computer invades the house and I have to be really conscious of that."

For Betsy, staying focused on the work at hand is hard. "I do think your work follows you around the house. It's hard for some people, including me, to stay on task when I'm thinking more about the laundry that needs washing instead of my deadline," she says. However, as a single parent, she needs to stay focused on completing her current projects and finding the next project to provide for her family. "For most people working from home, you don't have benefits and it sometimes is not a steady salary—your pay rises and falls on what you generate. I need to be pulling it together all the time to get the next project."

Despite the pressures of being a single mom, the ability to work from home and its flexibility is priceless, Betsy says. "Being able to be with your kids when you need to be is really special, as is having control of your work, and being entrepreneurial."

Denise Latimer
Inpatient Coder

"The biggest challenge for me is that people sometimes think that you really don't work since you work from home," says Denise Latimer, a single parent who works from home as an inpatient coder for a large hospital in Crystal, Minnesota. She stays home with her two sons, ages twenty-one and twelve, the oldest of whom is disabled.

She has a two-year degree as a health information technician, which helped her get her at-home job reviewing inpatient hospital stays to determine the diagnosis and procedures done during that stay. She used to work at the hospital, but five years ago began working from home doing the same job. "I had wanted to work from home for years but had to wait for the technology to catch up," says Denise.

"The advantages for working at home are endless, in my opinion," Denise asserts. Being home allows her to get her younger son off to school and to be home for him after school. "He loves to share about his day when he gets home, so I'm glad I'm here to listen," she says. She also doesn't have to purchase work clothes, doesn't incur extra expenses, puts fewer miles on the car, and can easily change her hours from day to day.

The few drawbacks include the difficulty of ignoring the chores that need to be done around the house while she's working and her inability to instantly consult her co-workers when she needs their input, she says.

Rebecca Jean Rivera
In-Home Childcare Provider

"There's a fine line between my home and my business—and sometimes no line," says Rebecca Jean Rivera, who provides in-home childcare in Atlantic Highlands, New Jersey, to two children in addition to her two boys ages four and nine. "You get no paid time off, no sick time, no break all day, and other people often think that I do not really work or that I do not work so hard. This job is hard and I work long hours. I am lucky if I get a five-minute break all day to sit down."

Rebecca's schedule involves watching the daycare children for ten hours a day, plus an additional two hours of paperwork and cleaning per week. She also spends about four hours in preschool preparation for the week on the weekends. She's been doing this for two years and wanted to be home with her own children as a single mom. "I get no breaks and am with my children twenty-four/seven. But I am home with my children and providing peace of mind to the parents of the children I care for. I love their kids and can share Christ with them as well as with my own children. That, to me, is a huge advantage."

Jennifer Smithfield
Mid-level Manager

Even before she was married and had a baby, Jennifer Smithfield worked from home. "When I was looking for a job, I was initially attracted to the company because the job description was unique and something I really wanted to do. However, the company was located in another state and I really didn't want to move," she says. "They were willing to consider hiring me as a remote employee—and the experiment worked. I'm still working for them and was even promoted to a management position."

Now living in Nashville, Tennessee, Jennifer's official title is Lead Analyst, Chemistry, which means she's a mid-level manager for a group of research analysts. "Basically, we retrieve information and deliver it to our clients in the form of research reports. While I'm technically a chemist, my research covers biology, chemistry, and agriculture. For the managerial portion of my job, I manage workloads and job distribution. I address quality issues both with clients and in-house staff. I interview potential new hires. I have also had to deal with disciplinary issues, although my supervisor is the actual 'hire/fire' person."

She works about fifty hours a week at her job, which she has been doing for five years. Her husband has been supportive of her at-home job, especially since she had been with the company before they were married. "It did take him a while to understand that, even though I was working at home, I wasn't going to be able to do daily chores during the workday," she says.

Working at home gives her more time to devote to other things because she has no commute. In addition, she saves money because of lower fuel and car maintenance bills, and because she has no need to have a full office wardrobe.

But being at home also means she is often stuck in the house without company for a while. "I feel lonely sometimes and miss the conveniences of being in the office, like the ability to completely end the work day when it's officially over," she says.

Jennifer also wants other Christian women to understand that while she's at home during the work week, she's working. "My experience has been unusual because I don't work for myself, I don't set my own hours, and I have limited vacation time," she says. "Even though I'm working at home, I'm still working—I can't do laundry or the dishes. Those things have to wait till the workday is over. I've had a hard time getting non-working women to understand why I can't join them for most weekday activities outside of standard church services."

It helps her to have a totally separate office that can be shut off from everything else so that she can leave her work space. "If I have my desk and papers out so I can see them, I would be working all the time," she says.

She would like other moms to think carefully about working from home before starting out. "I would stress that you need to know what you're getting into; you can't just assume it will be easy to work out everything. It's a lot easier to work from home with these advances from technology and it does provide a lot of opportunities—but unless it's for a company you've already worked for, don't become their first telecommuter."

Resources
Books

The Hidden Art of Homemaking
by Edith Schaeffer

The Mother At Home
by John S. C. Abbott

Woman at Home
by Arlene Cardozo

Online

Proverbs 31 Ministries
616-G Matthews-Mint Hill Road
Matthews, NC 28105
877-731-4663
704-849-2270
www.proverbs31.org
Encourages women through resources and a magazine, *P31 Woman.*

5

Pray, Research and Pray Some More

What you should do before getting started

After considering your family, financial, and personal situation, you need to think more specifically about the work you will be doing from home. I cannot emphasize enough the value of prayer before embarking on this endeavor. You should continue to seek the Lord as you go through these steps toward at-home employment.

As stay-at-home mom and entrepreneur Sandra Joseph relates, "While you may not make a lot of money at your home-based business, if you are doing what God calls you to do, then the satisfaction will follow.

"God always provides and takes care of you and your needs if you are doing what he calls you to do. It may not always be easy, but the benefits to your family and your emotional, physical, and spiritual health are numerous. Seeing my grown daughters walk with the Lord and follow his calling for their lives is so gratifying. I am so thankful that I was able to be home with them throughout their growing up years."

Simple arithmetic

As you continue to pray about working from home, write out the pluses and minuses of an at-home business. Jot down anything you can think of under each heading. Take several days to compile your lists. If you know other moms who work from home, ask for their input, too. The stories of mothers with at-home employment in this book can provide further insight into the pros and cons of working from home.

Advantages and Disadvantages of Working From Home	
Pros	Cons
Contribute to family income	Business expenses
Pay down debt	Income could fluctuate
Provide outlet for creativity	Isolation/loneliness
Flexible schedule	Hard to leave "work" behind
Be own boss	Interruptions from family
Able to be home with children	Having to stay focused on work when husband, children,
Professional career development	"Trapped" in house more
Helping others through job	Guilt over working
Volunteer opportunities	Less time for yourself
Generating clients/growing business	Pressure to succeed

Dealing with guilt

Terri Hughes, a medical transcriptionist who works in Gentry, Arkansas, says, "Staying committed to working scheduled hours has been an issue, because there are many distractions when you work from home. I have to keep in mind that the right thing to do is keep working because my employer expects it of me and because I'm to do my best at what I do."

Self-employment brings with it a host of issues generally not encountered in the office environment, such as taking on new financial responsibilities, generating clients or customers (marketing will be covered in chapter 10), monitoring work flow, motivating yourself to work, meeting deadlines, and filling out paperwork.

Just remember that while your job may require a set number of hours to complete the work required, you also may need extra time to keep up with the paperwork or to market your business to garner new customers or clients. Furthermore, you may need to schedule time to keep your skills or credentials up to date through classes or other kinds of professional development. These demands need to be considered when writing out the pros and cons of at-home work.

Seeking wise counsel

After you have a list of pros and cons, sit down with your husband and have a serious discussion about your potential at-home job. Waiting until the children are in bed or out of the house is wise, as you need to give your full attention to this meeting.

When you really want to do something, it's easy to dismiss the disadvantages in favor of the many advantages. I encourage you to look just as hard at the minuses as you do the pluses, because some days those minuses are going to seem insurmountable and cause a lot of stress as you work from home. When I consider a new freelance writing or editing assignment, I remind myself to think about how much time the project will take in light of my upcoming schedule, instead of zeroing in on the fee. It's better to have as realistic a view of the drawbacks as possible before launching a home-based business. Painting too rosy a picture can lead to unrealized expectations or frustrations down the line.

If you're single—or just want a second opinion—talk to a trusted advisor about the pros and cons of at-home employment. An older mom who has worked or is working from home can give you the ins and outs from the trenches.

If you already have an idea for what your home-based business will be, seek advice from a professional via an association or organization in the field you're considering. For general business advice, contact SCORE ("Counselors to America's Small Business") at *www.score.org*; SCORE members are available to talk with entrepreneurs of all types about starting a business.

"Many women seek a professional life as well as a family life," says Leslie Whelchel, an educational therapist who works out of her home in Potomac Falls, Virginia. "It has been challenging to manage both well, so getting advice from others is key to making this a success."

Lastly, contact your church for assistance. You and your husband might benefit from talking with your pastor or other church leader about your possible at-home work situation. Seeking godly counsel from Christian men and women can only enhance the decision-making process for you.

Once you have gathered input from all these sources, include the additional information from these friends, family, and brothers and sisters in Christ on your pros and cons list. Then take a few days to process and to pray about the list.

One note of caution: be careful not to be too impatient while going through these steps. The more thought you put into why and how you could manage to work from home, the easier the transition to at-home work and the smoother the process of working itself will be for you and your family.

If, after taking these initial steps outlined in the previous chapters, you feel that at-home employment is right for you, you're ready for the next step—choosing the right at-home business for you.

Terri Hughes
Medical Transcriptionist

Terri Hughes worked as an administrative assistant and legal secretary before embarking on her at-home career as a medical transcriptionist. As such, she converts physicians' dictation into typed medical reports for patients' charts.

For the past four years, starting before her two-year-old daughter was born, Terri has worked out of her home in Gentry, Arkansas. Since she started, her husband has been very supportive of her at-home employment, which takes about twenty hours a week to accomplish.

"I knew that when we had kids, I didn't want to put them in daycare, so I looked for an opportunity to work from home doing something I enjoy," she says. "I took a course in medical transcription and found a job within two weeks of completing the course."

After her daughter was born, her new daily routine changed her work schedule and subsequently her husband's as well. "I work when he's home, and he takes care of our daughter. However, that tends to cut into family time in the evening and reduces our time together as a couple."

Terri finds that she sometimes feels very isolated working at home. "It gets very lonely, and I've found myself becoming depressed at times," she confides. "Also, when you work at home and then spend a lot of time at home taking care of the kids, it feels like you just don't get out much. Your whole life is centered around your house. When my husband comes home from work, he's ready to be home and relax, and I'm ready to get out."

In addition, the numerous distractions of phone calls and family interruptions make it hard to concentrate on the task at hand. "Self-discipline is a must," Terri asserts. Setting boundaries between work and family can be a challenge. "Sometimes it can be hard to separate your work life from your family life when they are in the same location."

She's thankful that her job doesn't require daycare for her daughter, and the flexibility she has to take breaks and do a bit of housework or play with her child is wonderful. "During breaks, I can put a load of laundry in the washer, go for a walk outside, or just sit and relax on my couch."

Sandra Joseph
Entrepreneur

Sandra Joseph has been involved with many at-home businesses, starting in 1985 after the birth of her first daughter. Three daughters later, she still works from home as president of a Christian scrapbooking company. She has also written two books (*Scrapbooking Your Spiritual Journey* and *A Women's Ministry Guide to Scrapbooking*), speaks to women's groups, and is an independent subcontractor for a large Christian gift company. She lives with her husband and youngest child, now age fifteen, in Darlington, Pennsylvania. She logs anywhere from twenty-five to forty hours per week on her at-home businesses.

Sandra started her at-home career as a color consultant for a direct sales company, which she continued until 1992. Five years later, she started a small scrapbooking business in her home, later receiving a state grant to start a tri-state scrapbooking association encompassing Pennsylvania, Ohio, and West Virginia. Sandra used the grant funds to host a major scrapbook convention in Pittsburgh, Pennsylvania, and Columbus, Ohio, later selling her intellectual property for the association to another company.

Next, Sandra began working as a subcontractor for the same company as the national director of their scrapbooking association. She was the conceptual thinker for the company's national scrapbooking events and expo—all from her home office. Then, she and a partner started their own Christian scrapbooking company as a way to encourage Christians to explore and strengthen their own faith, and to pass on their faith in God to future generations through recording and remembering

God's faithfulness. Both of them work out of their homes to run the business.

"I initially decided to work from home to be with my daughters when they were small," says Sandra. "I continued to work at home to be involved in their school lives, and now I do it to be in control of my own time and to minister to women."

She values her husband's support of her many ventures. "He has helped me set up offices, babysat children, done bookwork, and encouraged me to follow the Lord's calling in my life even when the pay has not been there."

Having worked from home for more than twenty years, Sandra has seen a big shift in how women can work outside of an office. "The computer and, most importantly, the Internet make it so easy to connect with clients and business partners at a time that works for me and my time schedule," she says. "Just recently, I spent two and a half hours with a mom and her week-old baby and preschooler, and then I came home and worked late into the evening.

"The number-one word in my schedule has always been flexibility—I want to do what the Lord calls me to do that day."

Sandra does miss the camaraderie of working with other women in an office environment and sometimes misses not dressing up, because she says it "makes me feel good about myself."

But she does not allow housework to add more pressure to her workday. "I am fairly disciplined and organized, so I do not have problems with the distractions of home," she explains. "I will do laundry or start a meal while I work, but other household duties wait till the weekend or the evening."

While feeling isolated at times, Sandra's at-home work has enabled her to be open to "whomever and whatever the Lord brings into my life for that day. Every day for me looks different."

Leslie Whelchel
Educational Therapist

Leslie Whelchel's only regret about working from home as an educational therapist is that she did not start sooner. "I have two grown children and began working out of my home about six years ago while the youngest was still a teenager," she says. "But I could have done this much earlier if I had just thought about it."

The Potomac Falls, Virginia, mom has a background in teaching. She received her professional license to practice educational therapy, working with children who have been diagnosed with specific learning disabilities. Leslie spends about thirty hours a week meeting with clients in her home office.

"When I moved to Virginia seven years ago, I was seeking a profession which made use of my skills and yet would not take me away from home as much as my earlier professional life," says Leslie. She finished her master's of education and completed certification with the National Institute of Learning Development in order to work at home in this field.

"After teaching in a Christian school (my children attended the same Christian school), as well as working with a Christian nonprofit organization, I decided that it was still important to spend significant time with my family," she says of her decision to find at-home work. "It was important to make myself available to my children on the teenage and young adult side of child rearing."

One of Leslie's children has since returned home after a disabling accident.

Her husband helped her to realize how exhausting her former schedule had been, and he encouraged her to use their move to a new location as a good opportunity to reduce schedule demands and spend more time with the family and him. "He was a bit concerned that I wouldn't have my professional needs met with a stay-at-home job, but that has proven incorrect. My work is more interesting than I could have imagined.

He has become even more supportive as he has seen the positive impact on our family and my professional growth," says Leslie.

Leslie uses the extra time she formerly spent commuting to share breakfast time with her husband, and her flexible work schedule allows her to stay available to family members when needed. "While I have a set schedule of students and I don't allow intrusion from other sources, I am still 'in house.' I also can rearrange my schedule to meet the needs of other family members," she says, adding that she is no longer exhausted because of travel, ministry demands, or extra meetings relating to her job. "While my family has always come first in my heart and mind, I can put that into action by working from home."

To grow her business, Leslie has to generate clients through outside contacts and she often works late to meet the needs of students' after-school hours, making her day long at times. Some drawbacks to her working from home include not having built-in retirement and having to pay all of her professional expenses, like accreditation classes and supplies.

Leslie considers her private-practice educational therapy profession to be a ministry, as well as a source of income and professional fulfillment. "Having a profession has given me an opportunity to minister to not only my students, but to my church family, neighbors, and friends who have children with special needs. I have become a more accessible person now that I am not in a formal school situation. Additionally, I have extended myself professionally in a variety of settings through partnerships with schools and families while maintaining my office from home."

She encourages mothers to seek professions that can be developed into home businesses that complement the needs of family and meet professional and financial goals. "I am an advocate for people getting professional licenses," she says. "There are numerous professions that also lend themselves to home businesses for women."

Gigi Lehman
Freelance Writer and Editor

For twenty years, Gigi Lehman has put pen to paper, earning money as a freelance writer and editor, often working from home. "I wanted to contribute to the family income and to use my talents while still being the primary caregiver for my children," she says. She lives in San Antonio, Texas, with her two daughters, now teenagers, and husband.

Gigi schedules her fifteen hours a week of work around her home responsibilities, and cherishes the time she has to "transmit my own values to my children."

When her children were preschoolers, she had a teenager come for a few hours after school to watch the girls so that Gigi could conduct telephone interviews. But other challenges abounded. "You need to be able to think of at-home work as 'your office' and not be tempted to do housework during your work time. At the same time, you need to be able to psychologically 'leave work' and not go back to the computer or phone when you need to focus on your family or housework."

One of the positives for Gigi in working from home was helping the environment by not needing to commute to work. "I save money on parking, gas, and a work wardrobe. But most importantly, I'm able to spend time with my children," she says.

"My view of the Proverbs 31 woman is that she used her gifts to contribute to her family's financial well-being, as well as their physical, emotional, and spiritual well-being. I have two nearly-grown daughters and hope I have been a good example to them of using my gifts for the kingdom and for my family. Keeping my responsibilities as a wife and mother comes first—just as my husband, who works full-time outside the home, puts our family first.

"I have had Christian friends who spent as much time outside the home in Christian ministry as I did working outside the home part-time," Gigi says. "Twenty years ago, no one would think of being critical of a woman who spent her time volunteering in Christian causes, while a woman who spent an equal amount of time earning money sometimes felt that she had to justify the decision to other Christians."

Resources
Online

Homebodies
www.homebodies.org
Provides information and encouragement for stay-at-home mothers.

Mompreneurs Online
www.mompreneursonline.com
Provides advice and resource links about working from home.

Moms In Business Network
www.mibn.org
Provides an online, women-only network for working mothers.

SCORE
800-634-0245
www.score.org
Provides a host of resources for small businesses, including access to a variety of experts.

WebMomz
www.webmomz.com
Provides work-from-home resources.

Work-at-Home Mother
909 N. Sepulveda Blvd., 11th Floor
El Segundo, CA 90245
636-887-0337
www.wahm.com
An online magazine for at-home mothers who work from home.

U.S. Federal Government
www.business.gov
The official link to the U.S. government; provides information for small businesses.

Working Solo
PO Box 952
New Paltz, NY 12561
845-255-7171
www.workingsolo.com
wsoffice@workingsolo.com
Provides information and services for home-based business owners.

6

Turn Your Talents into At-Home Work

What should your business be?

ome-based businesses cover a wide range of jobs, such as baby blanket knitter, clothing mender, candle maker, copywriter, dog trainer, errand service runner, garage organizer, interior designer, jewelry maker, life coach, mystery shopper, nursery decorator, resume writer, and virtual assistant. The possibilities are endless! But how do you decide which home-based business or job might work for you?

Jobs of the future

First, let's take a brief look at some of the overall employment trends and which work-from-home jobs have future potential. The U.S. Department of Labor predicts that the "long-term shift from goods-producing to service-providing employment" will continue, with service-producing industries expected to generate more than three-quarters of all jobs in 2016.[16]

Behind these dry statistics lie lots of ideas for home-based businesses with great growth potential. In general, service businesses often fit into a stay-at-home mom's schedule and can be ideal for home-based businesses because they involve little or no inventory and have relatively low start-up costs.

With service-based work, many women have honed the skills necessary to be successful by simply serving their families, church, and communities. Many of the things you already excel at can be the basis for these service-based businesses.

Consider the following areas of job growth[17] and how those areas can translate into home-based businesses or work-from-home opportunities.

Education and health services: child-birth instructor, child-care provider, elder-care provider, massage therapist, medical transcriptionist, nanny-finding service, and tutor.

Professional and business: computer-repair/upgrade technician, IT solutions and maintenance engineer, and computer system and network security maintenance engineer.

Information: data processor, desktop publisher, editor, graphic artist, greeting-card writer, indexer, information broker, proofreader, software developer, website designer, and writer.

Leisure and hospitality: caterer, crafts maker, children's party planner, floral designer, gift basket designer, landscaper, personal chef, photographer, professional organizer, quilter, travel agent, and wedding planner.

Financial activities: accountant, architect, attorney, home inspector, real estate agent, real estate appraiser, and rental manager.

Other jobs with growth potential: actor, adult education instructor, computer engineer, database administrator, hair stylist, home-health aide, housecleaner, marketer, musician, personal trainer, registered nurse, teacher, technical writer, tour guide, web developer, and yard worker. See specific work from home careers on page 82 for more ideas.

Tami Conklin used her background as a public school math

teacher to launch an at-home job as a math tutor. "I had planned to go back to work after my son's birth, but the moment he was born, I realized I just couldn't leave him," she says. "I was already doing a bit of tutoring, so I decided to increase my tutoring hours and not go back to my previous job with a children's group."

Avoiding scams

When looking for a home-based business, you must be careful to avoid the many work-from-home scams that seek only to separate you from your money. Get-rich-quick schemes and easy-money promises abound, often camouflaged as legitimate businesses. The Federal Trade Commission estimates that work-at-home schemes defrauded 2.4 million people in 2005.[18] Scams come in all shapes and sizes, but most have the following characteristics:

■ Advertisements in newspapers, emails, and on websites that are not legitimate often offer little information. Here's an example: "Work at home—make $25/hr. You can earn a living from home. Start today." No information about the type of work or the company's name appears in the ad. Usually these ads are accompanied by a toll-free number or website address.

■ "No experience necessary" appears in nearly every come-on. Scams promise that you can do the work without possessing any particular skill or ability. Every legitimate job application asks for your particular skills or abilities, and working from home should be no different.

■ Work hours will be few but the payoff will be huge: "Earn $1,500-$4,000 weekly," promises this ad, emailed weekly to my inbox. Scams pledge big money in short time frames.

■ "Step-by-step training and support provided." This generally means you send in money to receive very generic information directing you to other organizations or information.

Common work-at-home scams include envelope stuffing, craft assembly, coupon clipping, compiling mailing lists, mail order fulfillment with another company's products, payment for reading books, calling 900 numbers, and multilevel marketing/pyramid schemes.

The Internet has spawned a new generation of these scams, complete with legitimate-looking websites, which target at-home mothers. These sites claim to offer "legitimate" opportunities, but instead hook you with the lure of a free trial for the job before asking for a "small" investment. These websites also give links to "featured listings" designed to snare unsuspecting browsers into "once-in-a-lifetime" opportunities to part with your hard-earned cash and personal information.

Be especially wary of online surveys, as they are a common way to scam consumers on the Internet. The hook is that these sites will pay you between five dollars and seventy-five dollars just to fill out simple online surveys from your home. The catch? You pay them for the "privilege" of filling out surveys for which you may or may not be qualified. Some of these online survey sites are legitimate, such as American Consumer Opinion, Beta Research, and Digital Research, Inc. Be careful, though, as it can be hard to distinguish between legitimate opportunities and scams.

"I won't pay for filling out surveys," says Andrea Spain, who lives in Mesa, Arizona, with her husband and seven-year-old daughter. Andrea has been taking online surveys for seven years, spending between ten and fifteen hours a week. "There are numerous survey companies that simply ask you to provide information about yourself (to see if you qualify to take the survey), but those companies do not require any money from you," she says.

If Andrea is filling out a survey that asks for too much personal information, such as tracking her phone calls or credit-card usage, she doesn't continue. She evaluates each survey based on its length and compensation. "If I'm going to take a survey for more than a half hour, it's not worth of my time unless I have good compensation," she says.

Your best defense against scams is to remember that anything that sounds too good to be true, probably is. Remember, while you may have start-up costs associated with launching your home-based business (e.g., purchasing computer equipment or inventory for making crafts), legitimate jobs that you apply for do not ask for upfront fees.

Real home-based business opportunities take time to get off the ground—so delete all emails offering you easy money for little work, avoid all websites enticing you to part with your cash and personal data, and ignore all ads promising you the job of your dreams. As Prov. 14:8 says, *The wise look ahead to see what is coming, but fools deceive themselves.*

Choosing what's best for you

Now that you've seen the job trends and are forearmed against scams, it's time to choose your home-based business. Take a minute to sit down and make a list of the things you enjoy doing the most. A good place to start is with your hobbies. Thinking back to what you enjoyed doing before you had children might bring the perfect job to mind.

Tiffany Mathias says she kind of fell into her business of creating video and DVD tributes using photographic and film media from her Reston, Virginia, home. A stay-at-home mother of three boys, Tiffany approached a friend with this idea after she created a video tribute for her parents' fiftieth wedding anniversary.

"The video was met with such pleasure and accolades by family, friends, and even the caterer, I made the suggestion to start a video tribute service together," she says. "Besides being great friends, we also complement each other in terms of the gifts we bring to the company—she is more detailed in her creativity and I'm more big-picture oriented and a risk taker."

Remember while writing your list that there are no silly ideas—and not everything you put down will translate into something profitable. For example, my mother and I love collecting seashells from the beaches of Sanibel Island, Florida, where we have vacationed as a family for several years. With boxes of these beautiful shells just lying around, we had an idea about six years ago to make crafts with seashells and sell them at a small, local arts-and-crafts festival. We had loads of fun thinking up ways to use the shells—from adorning photo frames and Christmas ornaments to decorating lamps and wreaths.

While we generally sell enough items to make a tiny profit, we will not be expanding to other festivals and craft shows. We've learned that this venture, while fun for us, will not be a big money-maker. (A good way to test the market with your business idea is to start small, such as selling items at a local crafts show or freelancing your work for little or no pay. Chapter 7 offers additional ways on how to conduct market research.)

But if your imagination needs a little jump-start to get those creative juices flowing, answer the following questions:

What do you do in your free time?

What do you long to do in your free time?

Before marriage and/or children, what were your dreams or goals?

If you had a job outside the home and liked it, could you transfer those skills to something home-based? (For example, teachers can become tutors, secretaries can work as word processors or transcriptionists, and accountants might find work as bookkeepers.)

Could your former employment be done at home?

What are your hobbies?

What are the clubs or organizations to which you belong?

Where do you volunteer?

What books do you like to read? Which sections do you browse in bookstores?

What do you do that prompts others to compliment you? Does your baking get rave reviews? Are you good at making invitations?

Which of your interests dovetail with current job trends?

If you have fun finger-painting with your toddler, you could organize paint-your-own-pottery classes; if you love pets, you could start a pet sitting or dog grooming service; if you enjoy organizing parties, you could become a party planner; if you love baking or cooking, you could cater; and if you enjoy working in your garden, you could sell herbs to local restaurants. The possibilities are limited only by your own imagination.

Christy Wolfe, a mother of three preschool-age children living in Centreville, Virginia, segued her office job with a government agency into an at-home job. She had the opportunity to test the waters of working from home while on bed rest during the last few months before the birth of her twins.

"I worked managing policy and development for the agency's deputy secretary," she says. "I already did a lot of work via email, so transitioning to working from home was fairly easy. I was able to negotiate a bill with Capitol Hill and the White House from my recliner at home." She works between seven and twenty hours a week at home reviewing policy for the department.

Where you live might dictate your choices for work-at-home employment. For instance, if you love animals and live in a rural community, you would have the space for animal breeding or boarding businesses, while an animal lover who lives in a more urban area would probably find many clients who need a dog walking service. Of course, the Internet and email have opened up numerous office-type jobs that can be accomplished no matter where you are located.

If you are still stumped, you could develop or polish skills by taking continuing education classes at your local college or university, or through your county's recreation department. Many professional organizations also offer workshops, training, and networking opportunities that might spark your creativity.

In addition, keeping in touch with former co-workers can lead to at-home job opportunities. Many of my freelance writing and editing assignments have come through former colleagues. If you are thinking of leaving your current job or have recently left an employer, make an effort to stay connected with your former boss and other associates. Even if you are not friends with them outside of the office, occasionally drop them an email about the company or something you know interests them. You might mention you saw a newspaper article about them or the company or that you like the redesigned company website. Don't forget to let your former co-workers know that you would be interested in at-home employment if appropriate.

Jenny Annoni got her at-home job as a project manager of information technology hardware and infrastructure for a chain of restaurants because someone she used to work with recruited her.

"I started working out of my home in Aliso Viejo, California, for the company before the birth of my son," she says. "After he was born, they asked if I would return to work and told me I could name my terms. So I told them I would work one hundred percent from the house, and have no requirements to attend on-site office meetings."

Staying in touch with former colleagues can open doors to at-home employment opportunities you haven't considered.

Refining your choices

Once you've answered the questions or made your list, go back and select two or three things you think might make a good home-based business. Now jot down all the ways those ideas could become a money-making venture for you. For example, if you enjoy cooking, you could start a home-based business as a personal chef (one who delivers home-cooked meals to clients' houses), a grocery-store shopper, a special-occasion baker, a caterer, or a menu planner. If you have received compliments on your homemade invitations, you could start a greeting card business, do custom-birth announcements, write personalized letters for children, or design wedding invitations.

"I've been sewing since the seventh grade," says Debbie Hufford, a seamstress and jewelry maker from Lancaster, Pennsylvania. "I've always looked at sewing as something I could do from home with kids." For several years now, Debbie has turned her love of sewing into a home-based business where she's made draperies and wedding party and bridal dresses and altered clothing while caring for her two young children.

After you've exhausted the job possibilities for your two or three main choices, it's time to narrow the field even further by choosing two jobs under each heading. For example, under cooking, pick personal chef and caterer; under homemade invitations, select custom-birth announcements and wedding invitations. Now you're ready for some feedback from family and friends.

Bounce these job ideas off your husband and a few close friends for their input on which one you should pursue. For example, your husband may remind you how stressed you got when cooking for the church seniors' dinner. Or your best friend could mention how much you enjoyed cooking meals for the family with a new baby. Even your children might have some good insights into what you should do—they may have a good understanding of what best suits your personality and talents. From their comments, you might deduce that becoming a personal chef would be more suited for you than becoming a caterer.

If you are having trouble deciding between your two or three choices, even after input from family and friends, then you can continue exploring these choices in the following chapter. Chapter 7 will help you list the initial steps for setting up your home-based business, from researching your chosen idea and finding a niche for your business to talking with other businesspeople and finding support groups.

So many options

In its January 10, 2007, edition[19] *Business Week* listed the top best home-based business ideas of 2007. The magazine talked with California-based Homestead Technologies, which designs and maintains websites for entrepreneurs, about its list of at-home business ideas. Homestead looked at business areas with a lot of spending and popularity, in addition to market trends and the level of difficulty in starting the business.

Homestead reported in the article that one of the best opportunities for the home-based business market is garage organization because of the growing trend in home makeovers, interior design and closet organizing.

"But the one area of the home that's not been focused on so far is the garage," said Manvinder Saraon, Homestead vice president of marketing and business development. "And garages of typical Americans tend to be very cluttered. So there's a market there, and it also presents easy entry: You don't need a specific degree to organize a garage. You're offering your skills and your time and hard work."

Homestead's other categories of growth in home-based businesses include selling on eBay; firm outsourcing for customer service, sales, human resources, doing background checks, and accounting; digital photography for scrapbookers; pet sitting; and children's art education, such as art, music, and drama classes.

Here is a list of job titles in which you can use your talents to develop an at-home business venture or employment opportunity.

Accountant

Actor

Adult education instructor

Animal boarder

Animal breeder

Architect

Attorney

Author

Baby blanket maker

Baker

Birth announcement creator

Bookkeeper

Breastfeeding consultant

Calligrapher

Cake decorator

Candle maker

Caterer

Chef

Childbirth instructor

Childcare assistant

Childcare provider

Children's party planner

Clothing mender

Columnist

Computer engineer

Computer-network maintenance engineer

Computer-repair/upgrade technician

Computer system maintenance engineer

Copywriter

Crafts maker

Database administrator

Data entry and processor

Direct sales representative

Dog daycare provider

Dog trainer

Dog walker

Doll maker and accessories

Desktop publisher

Dressmaker

eBay seller

Editor

Educational therapist

Eldercare provider

Environmental consultant

Errand runner

Event planner

Fashion designer

Floral designer

Furniture mover

Furniture refinisher

Garage organizer

Garage sale organizer

Gift basket creator

Gift wrapper

Graphic artist

Graphic designer

Greeting card illustrator and designer

Hair stylist

Herbs gardener and seller

Homegrown organic food packager

Home health aide

Home inspector

Home recruiter

House cleaner

Illustrator

Independent associate

Indexer

Information broker

Inpatient coder

Interior designer

Internal communications analyst

Internet book seller

IT solutions and maintenance engineer

Jellies and jam maker

Jewelry maker

Knitting instructor

Landscape architect

Legal transcriptionist

Life coach

Marketer

Massage therapist

Math tutor

Medical transcriptionist

Menu planner

Missionary recruiter

Mortgage broker

Musical instrument instructor

Mystery shopper

Nanny-finding consultant

Nonprofit consultant

Novelist

Nursery decorator

Office manager

Paint-your-own pottery owner

Personal chef

Personal shopper

Personal trainer

Personalized letter writer for children

Pet photographer

Pet sitter

Pet treat baker

Photographer

Picture framer

Policy reviewer

Potter

Production manager

Professional organizer

Proofreader

Public relations representative

Public speaker

Puppet maker

Quilt maker

Radio show host

Real estate agent

Real estate appraiser

Rental management agent

Research analyst manager

Registered nurse

Re-styler of wardrobes, jewelry

Resume writer

Rug maker

Scrapbook supplier/teacher

Scarf maker

Screen painter

Seamstress

Signmaker

Soap maker

Software developer

Speechwriter

Stencil maker

Teacher

Technical writer

Tour guide

Toy maker

Travel agent

Tutor

Video/DVD tribute creator

Virtual assistant

Weaver

Website designer

Website developer

Wedding planner

Worship director

Writer

Yard worker

Jenny Annoni
Computer Network Engineer

Before the birth of her son, Jenny Annoni worked full time as a computer network engineer and technical project manager. Three years ago, a former colleague recruited her to work for a quick-service chicken restaurant chain near her home in Aliso Viejo, California. She now works approximately ten hours a week managing the information technology hardware and infrastructure for the chain's new store openings.

"As the work I do is not on a regular schedule, i.e., emailing and answering phone calls, it is difficult to schedule specific things. My son, now seventeen months, always comes first. For example, I do not answer the phone if I am in the middle of reading him a book. Therefore, my days are very fluid."

Jenny finds it challenging working from home with a toddler, especially now that she is pregnant with her second child. "I have to decide between taking a nap and working. Sometimes, my son throws a fit while I am on a conference call," she explains. "Also, I'm sometimes not able to provide the same level of customer service in terms of responsiveness that I could before I had my son.

"It's difficult at times to deal with the constant pull in so many directions—mother, wife, job—and still find time to take care of yourself." To keep on top of her work, she has to make the time to do the work instead of letting it pile up each evening, but the advantage of being home with her son is what makes it all worth it.

Tami Conklin
Math Tutor

"My husband is thrilled that I found a way to work from home so we wouldn't need to put our children in daycare and so we could meet our financial obligations while still enjoying time together as a family," says Tami Conklin, who lives in

Herndon, Virginia, with her husband, two sons, ages five and sixteen months, and newborn daughter. "He's very supportive of my work schedule and does his best to help keep the house running smoothly."

Tami tapped her background as a public school math teacher to find a work-from-home job as a math tutor and mentor to other math tutors. For the past five years, she has spent between ten to thirty hours a week at her job.

"I feel my most important calling is to raise my children and teach them," says Tami. "Sometimes my work schedule can get in the way of that, and I'd love to just focus on my children exclusively. But financial responsibility is an issue as well—every Christian family has to find a way to balance financial obligations and family."

To balance her family time, she tries to have a few evenings each week where she doesn't work until after the children are in bed. Her daily schedule changes a lot because of her children's activities. "Luckily my job has a good amount of freedom in the schedule, so I'm able to fit my work time around my other activities. If I need to work when my husband is also at work, it is best if I have a mother's helper come in to keep the children entertained."

For Tami, her biggest challenge was helping her husband understand that her work really is work. "Just because I'm at home doesn't mean I can blow off my work. I have to set aside time where I'm just working, and the family has to respect that time."

Tami says she finds it difficult to keep up with their children, household, and work all at the same time. "Without my husband actively helping out every day, we just can't get it all done. He's great about helping, though, so we've been able to make it work."

Like other moms who work from home, Tami feels that work is "always calling me. I can always do more work since I'm right here, so it's easy to spend too much time on it. On the other hand, it's also easy to get behind and take it too casually, and then my family has to go on the back burner while I catch up."

She loves not having to worry about driving to and from work or needing to put her children in daycare. "I'm happy that even when I'm working, I am near my children and I know what they are doing. If someone bumps a head while I'm working, even if my husband or my mother's helper is 'in charge,' I can still kiss and make it better."

Debbie Hufford
Seamstress and Jewelry Maker

For Debbie Hufford, turning her love of sewing into a home-based business was an easy decision. Before having her first child, she worked as a costume designer and shop manager, making bridal veils on the side. Now with a five-year-old boy and a two-year-old girl, she works out of her Lancaster, Pennsylvania, home during the week, and on Saturdays, she works in a local art gallery designing jewelry.

She spends seven to ten hours a week on her various projects, which include making clothing and jewelry, and painting silk cloth.

Working from home was something Debbie had always thought about, especially since one of her college professors worked with her own youngsters by her side. "I just figured that was what I would do, and sewing and making jewelry is something that's relatively easy to do from home," she says.

Debbie's husband encourages her creativeness. "He thinks that I'm going to make us rich," she laughs. "But he's been very supportive of my desire to be in business."

The hardest part for her is separating her work space from the rest of the house. "My paperwork extends throughout the house," Debbie says. "I have a workroom on the third floor of our house, but because I use the washer and dryer in the basement a lot, things pretty much end up spread throughout the house."

Debbie also has trouble regulating the time that she needs to work from the time she can spend with her family and housework. "I get distracted," she admits. "It's harder for me because I am at home and I enjoy being with my family. It's hard to pull myself away to do my work, even though I love my work."

Debbie uses the time her children nap to work for an hour or two, running upstairs to her sewing room to work on projects. "It's sometimes difficult to divide the work time from the family time," she says. "It's so easy on Sundays to work because my husband is at home, but we want to remember the Lord's day without working, so I have to fit my work into other days."

She reminds other mothers, "It is not bad to ask for help with your kids. While Americans often think that you have to do everything yourself, you sometimes need extra help."

Tiffany Mathias
Video and DVD Editor

When Tiffany Mathias and a close friend decided to start a video editing company, she was excited that the work would enable her to stay at home with her three young boys. "Working at home was a better fit than trying to operate out of an office or with an organization," she says.

The two of them create video or DVD tributes for weddings, anniversaries, birthdays, and other special occasions using photographs and film materials. They also convert reel, 8mm, and VHS tapes to create digital archives for their clients.

From her Reston, Virginia, home, Tiffany logs up to thirty hours a week when she has a project. "The work dovetails nicely with my husband's interests in film and screenwriting, so I feel like I can be a more practically engaged helpmate in his dreams," she says. "I didn't really get involved for the money—though we do hope to be a profit-making company—but much more for the creative and relational opportunities."

One of her struggles is integrating her Christian faith with her work. "I'm still processing the integration of faith with this particular line of work," she says.

"As we're pulling people's stories together, we are finding it's a bit of an emotional journey for the family. There's a sense that we are connecting the threads of people's lives, and that has a reverent, sacred feeling that feels odd to market."

Her husband has been extremely supportive of her efforts because he sees how the creative outlet energizes her. Tiffany works on projects mainly while the children are sleeping, rising early and taking a short nap in the afternoon to enable her to work later at night.

"I don't want to take time away from family and household duties," she says. "I've always struggled with the pull of 'tasky' work—whether it is video editing or paying household bills—especially when I want to stop for the meaningful connection time with my kids. I'm sure the pull will intensify as our business grows."

For Tiffany, the challenges of working with interruptions from children and husband can be a major disadvantage. She also copes with living in a small house with limited space.

"My husband is a writer and working on creative projects on the side, so we have to fight for workspace," she says.

"We want home to be a place of rest and refuge, so making sure this goal is maintained even though work also takes place here is hard," says Tiffany. "I think this is the biggest challenge—keeping the distinction between the home and work duties that occur in the same space."

She states that she "wouldn't have gone looking for a job like this outside of the home, but the fact that I can do it from home makes it all possible."

Andrea Spain
Online Survey Taker

For the past seven years, Andrea Spain has given her opinion on a host of things, from which restaurants she frequents to what pet food she buys. From Mesa, Arizona, where she lives with her seven-year-old daughter and husband, she spends between ten and fifteen hours a week taking online surveys.

"I get a variety of things for filling out the surveys, such as cash, gift cards, and points redeemable for merchandise, such as hummingbird feeders," she says. She enjoys the chance to give her opinion, and carefully chooses which surveys to complete. "Some I make sure I finish right away, but the ones that enter you into a sweepstakes I usually don't rush to finish on time."

While she doesn't earn a lot of cash for doing the surveys, she likes trying products before they hit store shelves, such as new pet food and breakfast products.

Her favorite survey sites include ZoomPanel (*www.zoompanel.com*), PineCone Research (*www.pineconeresearch.com*), Greenfield Online (*www.greenfieldonline.com*), Ipsos North America (*www.ipsos-na.com/isay*), and Viewpoint Forum (*www.viewpointforum.com*).

"Through filling out these surveys, I have received hundreds of dollars in gift cards. I financed my patio door with Home Depot gift cards. I've tried many products, from PopTarts to granola bars to cat food to facial cream. If it's free, I'll take it," says Andrea. "I'm a substitute teacher, and when I'm not teaching, I'm doing surveys."

Andrea enjoys giving her opinion for a little something extra. "I get a little check in the mail every week, probably about twenty to thirty dollars a month," says Andrea. "Since I'm only working part-time at school, I have the time to do this and make some money."

Christy Wolfe
Policy Reviewer

Christy Wolfe did not plan her work-at-home experience—it was thrust upon her. Expecting twins, her doctor ordered her on bed rest for the final three months of her pregnancy. Of necessity, she transitioned her job with a government agency into a work-from-home situation.

"So much of work that I did was interacting with different sub-agencies within the department that were in completely different buildings, so even if I was in the office, I would not necessarily have face-to-face meetings with my colleagues," Christy states. Her job entailed a lot of reading and commenting on departmental policies, which could just as easily be accomplished at home. "I worked at home on bed rest, which went well," she says. "I think that helped play a role in demonstrating that I could work from home."

After the birth of her twin boys, Christy cut back to part-time work for the agency. Today, she works between seven and twenty hours a week from her home. "My supervisors and co-workers are happy to work with me working at home," she says.

With two-year-old twin boys and a one-year-old girl, Christy is more conscious of not overextending herself in relation to how much work she accepts. "I don't want to feel like I'm shortchanging my children, and I don't want all my free time tied up with work, so it's hard to strike a good balance. I never thought I would do any work when I was a mom, but I enjoy keeping up with what's going on in departmental policy."

Her husband, who also works from home as an associate pastor, was very supportive of her working from home. That gives her more flexibility to attend a few in-person meetings when necessary, she says. "I can work as little or as much as I want to from home because my boss is totally flexible."

Like other mothers who work from home, she struggles with drawing the line between working and taking care of the house and children. "Having your work stuff at home sort of bleeds into your home life," she says. "I try to keep work separate by leaving the bulk of my work to do when I have a babysitter or in the evenings."

A huge advantage of working at home for Christy is that she does not commute to work, which, from her home in Centreville, Virginia, to the agency in downtown Washington, D.C., took about two hours a day. "I also have total flexibility to make my at-home job work best for the family and not the office," she says.

While Christy enjoys her job, she tries to make time for herself each day, especially for devotions. She encourages other mothers to be disciplined about reading the Bible and other books that enrich our Christian faith. "I think as women, our minds tend to be all over the place, thinking about everything all the time. We need to be disciplined and have the energy to devote to reading to help develop our Christian walk."

Resources
Books

Discovering Your Natural Talents: How to Love What You Do and Do What You Love
by John Bradley and Jay Carty

How to Do What You Love for a Living
by Nancy Anderson

Online

All Work At Home Ideas
www.allworkathomeideas.com
Provides ideas and resources to start numerous at-home businesses.

Bizy Moms
www.bizymoms.com
Provides links and other resources for mothers.

CareerPlanner.com
Provides information about many careers for different life stages, plus online career tests.

Home-Based Working Moms
PO Box 1628
Spring, TX 77383-1628
www.hbwm.com
Provides support for mothers who work from home.

U.S. Department of Labor, Bureau of Labor Statistics
www.bls.gov/news.release/ecopro.toc.htm
Provides statistics and details on the job market.

7

Creating Your Mission

The critical first steps

N ow you're ready to begin establishing your home-based business. First, make sure your idea can be expressed clearly in fifty words or less in a "mission statement." Putting into succinct words what you want to do from home will help you focus your efforts in setting up your business.

Your mission statement should answer the questions: What is your business? What does your business do? What do you want to accomplish in your business?

The more detailed your mission statement, the easier it will be to find clients and establish your business. "I will teach children how to draw" would be a poorly written mission statement. A better, more focused mission statement would be: "In my in-home art studio, I will instruct children ages four to eleven on how to draw and construct pictures in oil paints, watercolors, finger paints, crayon, charcoal, and colored pencils." The second example provides a much clearer picture of exactly what you want to accomplish.

Once you have written your mission statement, read it to your husband, family members, and friends to make sure it clearly expresses your idea. As you continue to explore your at-home work idea, you may tweak or refine your mission statement, but for right now, your mission statement should give you a good foundation.

Digging deeper

Now it's time to begin researching the line of work you've chosen. Things to research include similar businesses to yours, demographic information about your target client base, prices of comparative items or services, and a list of start-up equipment and inventory. Instead of firing up your computer, I advise you to start by visiting your local library to check out books about your idea—this will save a lot of wasted time surfing unhelpful websites. Ask the reference librarian for assistance if you have trouble locating the right books. Also, see if there are magazines devoted to your topic.

After you have done a bit of library research, then you're ready to tackle the Internet. With the background you have gained from reliable sources, you will be in a much better position to wade through all the Web pages and sites out there on your topic and to zoom in on ones that are legitimate and helpful. Use a search engine like Google to do your initial searches. I also recommend finding out if there are any recent newspaper articles relating to your topic via Google News or Yahoo! News. These newspaper or magazine articles might list associations, organizations, or businesses related to your topic that will save you tons of time sifting through websites.

When you have questions concerning a company's reputation, check with the Better Business Bureau (*www.bbb.org*) to see about its legitimacy.

Find associations or organizations related to your field. These businesses can provide resources, tips, trends, and ideas on how to run your home-based business. For example, say your idea is to start selling homemade doggie treats. Typing "Pet products" into the Google search engine brings up a list of pet stores and the American Pet Products Manufacturers Association, which has a vast array of statistics on the growth of pet products, as well as providing links to other helpful sites, such as the Pet Food Institute.

"I started exploring all my options while I was pregnant with my first child," says Elizabeth Anne Tappan, a mother of two who lives in Richmond, Virginia. "I thought about a lot of different options and eventually settled on medical transcription through advice from another mother in our church." The online course, which she completed in three months, cost about fifteen hundred dollars, and she found a job right away. "It was hard at first, and because I was new and slow, the pay was low at first. But within six months I was at ease with my profession and I was making a great income."

Who's your competition?

With your background research complete, it's time to check out the competition. Look in the local yellow pages or contact your Chamber of Commerce to find out what types of similar businesses already exist in your area. Stop by, call, or look online to see what services they offer.

Consider shadowing a professional who does the same or a similar job for a few hours or an entire day. Most professionals, as long as you make it clear you are not there to influence potential clients to come to your business, are happy to show new entrepreneurs a behind-the-scenes look at their business. If there's not a similar business in your area, look for one in a neighboring city or even state. The proprietors in that area might be more willing to talk with you on the phone about the pros and cons of running such a business without the risk of helping the competition.

Research, research, research

With the initial research into the competition under your belt, you need to determine what type of niche in the market you will fill. Remember that market research does not have to be expensive or complex, but it is a necessary, and even fun, step.

Bounce ideas off of friends for how your service might differ from the competition. Conduct your own informal focus groups with people to whom you would like to market your services or products.

For example, if you're interested in offering children's art classes, you might "borrow" a few kids from church or the neighborhood (with parental permission, of course!) to see what approach they like best. Bring supplies so that they can experiment with the different mediums you are considering teaching, such as charcoal pencils or pottery. The information you gain from a focus group could help you tailor your class offering to specific age groups. Meet with several different focus groups encompassing the same ages to get a good understanding of their thoughts.

Next, you need to discover how big your particular client base could be. If you live in a small town, you might not find enough people who want to learn basket weaving to sustain a business, but a larger community might provide a bigger pool of potential students.

Look at published directories, such as Thomson Gale Directories. These directories list associations, organizations, and companies, among other job-related research. Again, consult a reference librarian for more resources along this nature. For research purposes, it is not necessary to purchase these directories. If your library doesn't have a copy of the directory you need, ask about inter-library loans. Also check with local college and university libraries to see if you could look at the volume on-site. Many libraries have access to computerized databases that could provide statistical and demographic breakdowns.

To find out your area's demographic breakdown, start with city hall or the county seat. The U.S. Census Bureau (*www.census.gov*), the U.S. Department of Commerce (*www.commerce.gov*), and the U.S. Small Business Administration (*www.sba.gov*) will have some of this type of information, but you are probably better off starting locally. If your home-based business will target a specific population, such as retirees or preschool children, ask your local government if they can break down the numbers for that demographic category including age, gender, income, and education level. Associations and organizations also might be able to assist with big picture numbers—such as national, state-by-state, and large metropolitan areas—and the growth potential for your idea.

The demographic information will help you to develop a profile of your typical customer, which will assist you in developing marketing materials, logos, products, and so on. For example, for a pet-sitting business, you would search for demographic data concerning how many people within a certain radius or area own pets. Using those stats you would want to break down that pet-owning population by income level to identify the most likely number of potential clients.

Find your niche

Increasingly, Americans want personalization for a wide-range of services, which can be a good thing for those just waiting to fulfill a need with a service or product. Many consumers want items or services tailored specifically to their needs or desires. We are moving away from mass-market goods, and now favor specialty items.

Finding a niche for your home-based business could be fairly easy, or it could take some serious thought. For instance, if you love to bake and want your at-home business to involve baking, you probably realize you need to specialize in something to stand out from the pack.

For instance, you might choose cookies as your specialty. Further customize your business by offering a personalized cookie service that would use the client's family recipe for the cookies. Or devise cookie birthday or holiday gift baskets with appropriate flavors, such as pumpkin for Halloween and marshmallow chocolate for Easter. Another way to customize your business would be to bake "cookies" for dogs or cats.

Use your imagination to think outside the box and come up with several variations on your idea. Take into consideration the market research you have done to see how each variation would gain or lose part of the client base you plan on targeting.

Volunteer your time

Another way to test your idea is to provide your services or product free for groups in your target demographic. For instance, if your idea is children's art classes, donate tuition for one of your classes to your local elementary school's auction. Sign up to teach one class for free through your local recreational center or educational services.

Business contacts can be made by offering to do a free seminar on your topic for local business clubs, churches, or the senior center. If it's not too costly, get a booth at a local arts-and-crafts festival to see how your products sell.

In addition, try something once before committing to a longer-term assignment. Take on a project on a trial basis of a week or month before agreeing to a longer one.

Paula Sokody Wilding was teaching evening courses for a college when the English Department and online course manager asked her to design and teach an online English course. She agreed to try one class, which proved successful enough that she added a second online course a year ago. "My husband was simultaneously working full-time and attending law school in the evenings, and we did not believe I could be away from home and our young daughter any more than the few nights I taught class. The Lord knew my desire to be at home with my children and blessed me with an opportunity to make money, do something I love, and exercise my brain," says the mother of three, who lives in Wheaton, Illinois.

Support help

The last thing you need to do before officially getting your business up and running is to gather a support group. You need to have others with whom you can share your frustrations and successes. This group includes family members, peers, church members, close friends, neighborhood moms, or online discussion group buddies.

Having such a group will help keep you going when things get rough and help keep you humble when you find success. Call on whomever you can for prayer and encouragement for when you encounter roadblocks. Share the joys as well as the sorrows with these friends and family. Working at home can be lonely at times, and you need to take the time to reach out to friends and family to keep you going. (Chapter 11 will provide more ideas on how to juggle family, friends, and me-time.) I joined a local Christian writer's group that holds meetings once a month. It's a great encouragement to me when I've struggled with my writing, and a wonderful way to share my successes.

Overcoming obstacles

When you do run into obstacles—and you will—remember to take a step back, pray, and evaluate if that roadblock is God's way of closing that particular door. You might get all fired up about a great idea, but after conducting this research, you may decide it's not for you after all.

If that's the case, please do not be discouraged. Sometimes, in God's infinite wisdom, he closes doors we thought should be open. But I believe that it is always better to have tried than to wonder "what if." Perhaps you need to shelve this idea for a while; perhaps it's not the job for you; or perhaps you need to refine it to see if it fits another way.

One roadblock you might encounter is finding similar businesses in your area or a smaller-than-expected client base. About twelve years ago, a friend and I had an idea for a Christian radio show about singles. Single ourselves at the time, we conducted market research, wrote up a proposal, and even pitched the idea to someone in radio. But the show never got beyond those plans despite our best efforts. We concluded that being radio personalities wasn't in our future. But I was glad we had thoroughly explored the idea, as we learned how to write a proposal and present our idea. While not successful, we always would have wondered "what if?" We were happy to have had the chance to fully explore the idea, even though the show never aired.

"I'm not sure that my two jobs as a breastfeeding counselor and as a volunteer coordinator are the best fit," confides Toni

Lane, a mother of four in Aitkin, Minnesota. "But at the same time I trust that God can and will lead me out of them and into something different when the time is right. What a blessing to know that it doesn't all depend on me figuring it out by myself!"

Now that you have written a succinct mission statement, completed the initial research into your business' potential and gathered together your support team, you are ready to set up your business. 🏠

Toni Lane
Breastfeeding Counselor

When Toni Lane needed extra income to supplement her husband's salary, she turned her background as a registered nurse into an at-home job as a breastfeeding counselor. As such, she helps mothers involved in a government assistance program with breastfeeding questions and concerns. She also works part-time as a volunteer coordinator for seniors, matching people age fifty-five and older who are interested in volunteering with nonprofit organizations looking for unpaid assistance.

The Aitkin, Minnesota, mother of five homeschools her four youngest children, ages ten, eight, four, and two, in addition to spending between ten and twenty hours a week on her two part-time at-home jobs. "The hardest part for me is establishing priorities," says Toni. "It's hard to have enough time to put toward what is most important for us, which is training up the next generation by homeschooling."

Her part-time work tends to take out whatever margin of time she has left after her teaching and housework, she says. But, she feels that working from home allows her the freedom to raise and teach her children "in the training and admonition of the Lord" without having to resort to daycare. The challenge for Toni is "discerning between the urgent and important, and the not-so-important, as well as being flexible."

In addition to her homeschooling and part-time jobs, she

also volunteers for numerous activities at her church. "Life is wonderful, and God is teaching me precious things during this very busy time of life. But I am really trying to evaluate my use of time. The busier I get, the more I tend to forget who is in charge. I ask the Lord to help me to use my time wisely and to establish the work of my hands."

She wants other Christian mothers to see that working from home isn't always easy but it's very much worth it. "Pray about it," advises Toni. "God is a God of miracles, and if he wants you home with your children, he is very capable of pulling those details together for you and your family."

Elizabeth Anne Tappan
Medical Transcriptionist

While pregnant with her first child, Elizabeth Anne Tappan of Richmond, Virginia, began planning her exodus from the workplace to at-home employment by investigating her options, ultimately settling on medical transcription. "We were newlyweds, both just out of school, and we did not have the financial resources for a new baby—he was a honeymoon baby and completely unplanned," explains Elizabeth. "We both felt strongly about not placing a newborn into daycare, so I looked around for something I could do at home with him."

She started her at-home career after completing a course in medical transcription when her oldest child was four months old. Now the mother of a two-year-old son and a newborn daughter, Elizabeth logs between fifteen and twenty hours a week typing dictated doctor's notes into formal reports.

A former geologist and environmental laboratory analyst, Elizabeth is grateful she found a job she can do at home. "I know God provides what we need when we need it. This is an experience that God will ultimately use to benefit my family and me spiritually," she says. While ideally she would like to not work at all, she finds this at-home work a good compromise. "I know my family is a priority over my work, but that isn't always realistic in a society that almost always requires a dual income," she explains.

Her husband was completely supportive of her decision to find at-home employment. "He was very nervous about supporting us on just his income, and he was relieved that I was willing to help out in that regard. It has made our relationship much stronger, because he knows I am there for him in all of life's challenges and that my expectations are realistic, even if the situation doesn't initially appear ideal. He was also very happy that we were able to find a way to keep our children home."

Eventually, the couple hopes to eliminate the need for Elizabeth's income, but she is grateful that God has "showered us with blessings whenever we needed them. ... I know God has helped both of us grow tremendously through our current situation. I always tell other engaged couples not to fear the unexpected—like having a baby right away—because God will bless them in so many ways and take care of the small details when they just follow his plan. Every time my husband or I have needed an increase in income, time off, or better working conditions, God has provided it without fail. It never ceases to amaze me how our needs are met. In just the three short years we have been married, our household income has doubled, even though I work significantly less as a stay-at-home mom and my husband has not increased his workload at all."

Her daily schedule starts early in the morning in order to have quiet time to work. "I have to get up at five-thirty in the morning instead of sleeping until my son gets up two hours later. I rely on naptime to do work, so naps for me or contemplative times are not options. I have to do all the cooking, cleaning, errands, and so on, while my children are awake, since I work when they sleep. I also have to make sure I devote some time to them during their waking hours," she says. Occasionally, she has to work when her husband is home from his job, but her daily routine is effective and she is able to spend time with her husband in the evenings.

With a packed schedule, she does struggle with feeling tired. "I feel like I have to do it all without any help from anyone else. I don't have any childcare or housekeeping service to help me. It's just me and my husband, so sometimes I wish I had less to do in the day."

Because she's an independent contractor, she plans very carefully for vacations. "I don't get paid vacation or sick days, and when you own something like a business, you tend to take less time away. I feel very responsible for my work and have a hard time taking time off because of feelings of obligation towards the company. I have to make God, family, and myself a priority, otherwise I would always be thinking in terms of lost income during holidays and vacation," says Elizabeth.

But the advantages outweigh any negatives. For example, she doesn't need a car, a work wardrobe, or childcare. Her only business expenses are her computer and a high-speed Internet connection. She has a twenty-four hour turnaround time per assignment, so her hours change on a daily basis. "This flexibility is essential for sick kids, short nap days, and all the other unexpected things that can come up in a day. I get to be my own boss, set my own hours, and eat when I'm hungry."

Her income enables them to afford a better lifestyle, eat healthier, and pay for dental care, in addition to things she feels are important to the development and health of the children. "I also have the security of knowing that if anything ever happened to my husband, my daily life would not change in the financial realm," says Elizabeth. "I wouldn't have to suddenly find work or put my kids in daycare or change the way I run my day. I would have an adequate income and the flexibility to be a stay-at-home mom."

She adds, "I know God can do so much with circumstances like working from home, and I think it is great that more moms are able to find ways both to be a mom and work from home. I know from personal experience that God blesses us for taking on the challenges we face, and he uses any suffering or struggles to bring us closer to him."

Paula Sokody Wilding
Online Teacher

Paula Sokody Wilding was teaching evening English courses in a college classroom when the school asked her to develop and teach an online literature course. Three years later, she teaches two online courses, one she designed from scratch and the other she adapted from a correspondence course.

"I feel that the Lord blessed me with an amazing opportunity," says the mother of three children, ages seven, two, and seven months. "I have many friends who wish they had the same situation as I have. I am able to balance my first job of being a mom with an additional job that challenges me mentally and provides extra income. The college I teach for is a Christian college and has been very understanding of my situation."

While the extra income she earns is welcome, her husband encourages Paula to work because of its importance to her. "He knows that it helps me feel more like myself and not just being defined by my children or home. Those things are extremely important to me, but they seemed to have taken over much of my individual self over the years. He is very supportive of my current work, as I hope to turn it into more of a full-time career after my children are much older," says Paula, who lives in Wheaton, Illinois.

She has to focus diligently when she's working. "I have a smaller amount of time available for work, so it must be spent well and productively," she explains. "I do feel torn at times between my children, my home, and my job. I try to focus on my work when the kids are at school or asleep but it is not always possible. Since they are used to me being available, it can be frustrating to them that I am visible, but not available, and frustrating for me as I may not be able to focus on my work. There also are times when I set aside time to work and end up cleaning the home, spending time with my husband, or just relaxing from a busy day."

Even as an at-home mother who's available to her children, Paula struggles with some of what she calls the "working mom's guilt." "I want to dedicate myself to my children, and yet I feel that pull between not only my children and my job, but my household, friends, family, and husband. It is a difficult balance, and one any woman must face. It is just a different animal when all the components one must balance are located in the same space."

However, she takes pleasure in being home for her children, her first job, she says. "I would not continue working if my first job suffered too greatly because of my paying job. Also, my children see that while they are my most important job, I am not solely 'mom'; I have responsibilities and gifts outside of them and their needs. I hope it is a positive image for my children to see their mom dedicated to them, but also a mother who uses her abilities in other ways as well."

She would stress to other women considering at-home work opportunities to pray with their husbands about the possibilities. "I am proof that the Lord can answer the desire of one's heart. I believe he can provide opportunities for women who want to dedicate their lives to raising their children at home. Even with all the stress and difficulties of balancing this life, I would not design another for myself."

Margarita Muzzall
Relationship Manager

"I have a sense of calling," says Margarita Muzzall, who, after the birth of her first child, worked from home temporarily. "I knew that I had a great responsibility and opportunity to raise my son, while at the same time, I had the desire to pursue a career outside the home. Working from home seemed to satisfy both."

Before she had her first child, Margarita was a relationship manager underwriting commercial real estate loans to healthcare businesses. She had gone back to work after the birth of her son, but the nanny she had arranged to watch him quit without notice. Her sister came to help and after a while, Margarita and her husband decided it would be better for their son if she stayed home for a time. "When I presented the decision at work, we agreed that I would work from home until they found a replacement," says Margarita, who lives in Arlington, Virginia.

She worked about thirty hours a week for four months before the company found a replacement and she quit working for a while. "My husband was ready for me to quit my job much sooner than I was. Working from home was a compromise."

She enjoyed working from home and liked the fact that she didn't have to get ready for work or commute. "That gave me a bit more freedom early in the morning and evening to make breakfast and dinner for the family," says Margarita. "Of course, I spent more time in the 'off hours' dedicated to work, such as late in the evening and during naps."

While she felt that she did the job as well as she did in the office, the hardest part of working from home was that her boss just did not like her being out of the office. "As he put it, 'I cannot say our clients have felt the difference, or that the work is not being done, but I am just not comfortable with it.' Of course, the networking and maintaining relationships with the office was a challenge, too. A lot of time on the phone was used to keep in touch," she says.

One drawback to working from home for Margarita was being below the radar of senior management. "At the same time, it seemed to limit the options. You are not going to apply for that big promotion now that you are not at the office anymore."

But she loved the ability to continue to care for her child, see his development and raise him, while still maintaining her career.

Resources
Books

Market Research Made Easy
by Margaret Doman and Dell Dennison

*Marketing Research That Won't Break the Bank: A Practical Guide
to Getting the Information You Need*
by Alan R. Andreasen

*The Market Research Toolbox: A Concise Guide for Beginners,
Second Edition*
by Edward F. McQuarrie

Online

Better Business Bureau
www.bbb.org
Provides information on the reliability of companies.

eMarketer
75 Broad Street
32nd Floor
New York, NY 10004
212-763-6010
800-405-0844
www.emarketer.com
Provides Internet statistics and reports.

EntreWorld
www.entreworld.com
Offers a list of more than a thousand Web resources for small businesses.

Thomson Gale
800-877-4253
www.gale.com
Creates and maintains more than 600 databases that are published online,
in print, as eBooks, and in microform.

U.S. Census Bureau
301-763-4636 (for questions about data)
www.census.gov
Provides statistics and data on the American population.

U.S. Department of Commerce
1401 Constitution Ave., NW
Washington, DC 20230
202-482-2000
www.commerce.gov
Provides information relating to commerce.

U.S. Small Business Administration
800-827-5722
www.sba.gov
answerdesk@sba.gov
Provides a wealth of information about operating small businesses.

Chapter **8**

You're Ready...Get Started!

How should you set up your business?

You've completed the initial steps—now it's time to create a business plan, calculate start-up costs, and set up your home office.

What's in a name?

If you are going to be selling a product or service, you'll want to come up with a name for your at-home business. (If you are a freelancer, just use your name as your business name.) Jot down some ideas, but try to avoid being too clever or cute. You want the name to stand out and accurately describe your services or products, and being too inventive might leave potential clients wondering what exactly you do.

For example, if your business is running errands, you could call it *Running for You* or *In a Pinch*. After coming up with two or three names, check the phone book to see if another company has the same or similar-sounding name. Try out the name with family and friends to gauge reactions and tweak as needed.

Shakespeare might have wondered what's in a name, but for many companies, their name is the most important part of their business. Take care in coming up with yours.

Doing business as

If you use a fictitious name for your business, then you need to file a DBA/Fictitious Business Name Certificate. DBA stands for "doing business as"—under what name you will operate your business. If you are going to be an LLC or corporation, you might not need to file a separate dba form, but check with your county or city clerk's office. Also, if you add anything after your name, like "Sons" or "Company," then you should file a dba. Some states do require a dba even if you use your legal name as your business name. Contact your county clerk's office or the local chapter of the Better Business Bureau for more information.

Basically, dbas provide you with the ability to enforce contracts signed under your business name and to apply for the necessary permits or licenses relating to your business. Dbas also help local, state, and federal governments keep track of companies in case of complaints or legal problems.

Registering for a dba is simple. Your county or city clerk where you plan to do business can provide the necessary forms and fees, which are usually minimal. Once you have filed a dba, you can operate under your business name, such as opening a business checking account, depositing checks made out to your business name, applying for a business or seller's license, or advertising your business.

Putting plan to paper

Developing a well-written business plan is key to any successful venture. This will help you immensely as you plan your business. Use your mission statement as the basis for your business plan. Potential investors or loan officers usually require a detailed business plan before investing or lending money for start-up costs. Certain types of loans require a detailed business plan. Many resources exist for writing a business plan, such as SCORE and local Small Business Development Centers, but here's an overview of what one entails, in addition to your mission statement:

Summary. This should run two pages and explain your business—its activities, key objectives, and goals.

Market research. This should be your largest section. Mention your competition. Include how your product or service will differ from the competition. Draw a clear picture of who your clients will be, and give statistics showing numbers and growth potential (this can be as simple as using population projections for your city or business area). Your growth potential can also include your ideas for expansion beyond a certain group of clients or people. For example, marketing your pet biscuits to dog owners who frequent local dog parks is your initial market, but your plans for growth might include expanding to area pet stores and dog grooming salons. Use the research you gathered in chapter 7 as the basis for this exercise.

Actual product or service. Provide a detailed explanation of your product or service.

Sales. Describe how you will sell your product or service. Talk about the ways to reach your client base, such as your advertising plan, trade show attendance, website presence, partnerships with other companies, and so on.

Staffing. Explain how your business will be staffed and managed. Include a brief biography—one paragraph is sufficient—of the key personnel: you, partners, and other important team members, if applicable.

Financial data. Include balance sheets, profit-and-loss statements, cash-flow analysis, and a break-even chart. Consult an accountant for assistance in compiling this data. For most, this will not be necessary, given the small nature of your business. This financial data will give you some idea as to what you will need if your business grows.

Investment opportunities. List what an investor will receive in return for providing funds.

Addendums. Put research information and miscellaneous charts, graphs, and tables relating to your business here.

Your entire business plan probably will run between ten and forty pages—the more formal the plan, the longer it will be.

Establishing ownership

Depending on your business model, you will need to structure your business—especially one that has growth potential. You have four basic options: sole proprietorship, partnership, incorporation, and limited liability company (LLC). This is one area you should consult with an an attorney for clarification and advice.

A freelance or contractual worker—one who does work on a per assignment basis—generally does not need to formalize ownership to operate. If you work for a company at home, you will not need to establish legal ownership.

The simplest—and most likely the best for you—is sole proprietorship, which means that the owner and business are one and the same. This is generally a service business with you as owner providing the service. If you're starting out small, in most cases this is probably your best the option. (This also means that you will file your business and personal taxes together—see chapter 9 for more details.)

A partnership involves more than one owner with profits and losses divided among the participants. Attorneys, doctors, and other professional service providers generally form partnership businesses.

Incorporating encompasses businesses with employees, and financing from a bank. Owned by shareholders, a corporation is chartered by the state.

An LLC is a state-chartered organization that has a reduced personal liability, similar to a corporation, but provides the tax advantages of a partnership or sub chapter "S" corporation.

Start-up costs

After you have created your business plan and decided on a formal structure, you should think about what funds you will need to get started.

First, list everything you will need to run your business: computer equipment, software and Internet connection; separate phone or fax lines and fax machines; copiers, business cards and general office supplies. Also, list anything you will need to provide your service, such as cleaning supplies, or to manufacture your product, such as baking ingredients.

Next, estimate the cost of buying or installing the items you need, including any computer upgrades, electrical work, phone line installation, or other professional services. From that list create a budget or spending plan, outlining what you need now and approximately how much it will cost. Include monthly expenditures, too, such as Internet access fees or cell phone plans. Add to that budget any costs associated with marketing your business. Don't forget to include the estimated price of potential repairs or services. Incorporate the cost of any childcare that might be needed for you to work from home.

If your profession requires certification or courses, itemize the costs associated with that training into your spending plan. You might want to start the certification process as soon as possible in order to be ready to begin working when all your other preparations are completed.

Sometimes, employers will pay for certain monthly expenses for their telecommuting employees. For example, Melissa Jenkins of Harrisonburg, Virginia, works for a children's organization about twenty hours per week. She goes into the office two mornings a week and completes the remaining hours at home. "My employer paid for my Internet connection and provided access to the office network from my home," she says, which helped her make the decision to move home.

From her Brandon, Mississippi, home, Sherry Lanier works as a database administrator for a seminary. She is thankful that she doesn't have to worry about finding her own tech support. "It was a really easy transition for me," says this mother who started working from home when her daughter was a teenager. "I'm fortunate that the head of the seminary's computer department literally lives down the street from me. So if I have any computer issues, he just stops by and fixes it."

Your fee structure

Now you're ready to determine what to charge for your services or products. Your market research should have given you a good idea of what the competition is charging for the same or similar products or services.

Be careful not to over- or under-value your service or product. When thinking about price setting, add the cost of supplies plus the cost of your time.

Start at an hourly rate for your time and supplies, then estimate how many hours you will spend on the project. If you will be driving to clients' homes, include gasoline costs in your pricing by estimating distances to arrive at an overall figure.

For example, say you have a pet-sitting service and your target client base is within a ten mile radius of your home. You determine gasoline expenses will run about a gallon per visit round trip. Your service includes spending two, thirty minute visits per day with the pet, excluding travel time.

A competing service offers one, forty-five minute daily visit for thirty dollars. You decide to charge fifty dollars for the two half-hour visits, which breaks down to twenty-five dollars per thirty minutes.

You also decide to give a small discount for contracts longer than a week, such as "sign up for ten daily visits and the eleventh one is half off" to garner repeat clients.

You may need to adjust this figure up or down, depending on the amount of work you get. For instance, pet-sitters might want to increase prices modestly during the summer months when they will probably be busier with vacationers needing care for their pets.

Setting up your home office

Whatever your home-based business, you will need an office—some set place where you can perform your business-related tasks, such as doing paperwork, processing payments, or meeting with clients. This does not have to be a separate room—a corner of the family room, the kitchen breakfast nook, or part of the guest bedroom can be re-configured as your office space. Decorate the area in a way that makes you feel comfortable and productive, adding whatever touches will make it your own workspace.

Once you have designated an office space, you need to figure out the minimum requirements for office furniture and equipment, such as a computer desk or hutch, chair, filing cabinet, desktop or laptop computer, telephone with answering machine, fax machine, copier, printer, and so on.

While you may covet that cherry wood executive's desk, you probably do not really need high-end office furniture. Search garage sales, thrift stores, consignment shops, online sites like *www.CraigsList.org*, and newspaper classifieds for inexpensive furniture and equipment. Just because you get something second-hand doesn't mean it's junky. I bought my four-drawer black metal filing cabinet from a Craigs List ad for only ten dollars. It has only a few minor nicks and scratches that are hardly noticeable.

Other places to acquire good used office equipment and furnishings are from companies that are upgrading their offices. Ask family and friends to let you know when their company purchases new office equipment because most of the time, the company will either give away the old stuff or sell it at a huge discount to employees. One association I worked for upgraded the entire staff's computers. The old models, which were still working, were sold for under a hundred dollars to any employee who wanted one.

Keep in mind that some office equipment, such as a fax machine or telephone, does not need to be new to serve your needs. My in-laws, who own a real estate business, gave us their old thermal paper fax machine a few years ago when they upgraded to a plain paper model. In my business, I rarely send or receive faxes, but occasionally have needed to do so. Having an older fax machine doesn't hamper my ability to conduct business, and it saved us some money. However, if you use the equipment daily or weekly, buying it new might be a good investment.

Also consider purchasing inexpensive (or downloading for free) software that allows sending and receiving faxes on your computer. A scanner/copier/printer combination might be perfect for a business that requires limited copying, too.

Some employers will provide office equipment to their telecommuting employees. Tina Simpson's employer, the missionary arm of a Protestant denomination in Atlanta, Georgia, wanted her to continue working for them as a missionary recruiter after the birth of her first child and helped set up her home office. "I went to my boss when I was about five months pregnant with our first child and told him I was expecting, so he would probably want to go ahead and start looking for another recruiter," Tina says. "He said, 'Well, you're not quitting!' And I said, 'Well, no one else is going to take care of my children.' A few months later, I was set up at home with a phone, computer, printer, desk, chair, file cabinet, etc."

One expense that might seem negotiable at first is getting a separate phone line or cell phone for business calls. However, if you anticipate needing to make or receive a lot of calls—or want to know when the phone call is business or a friend—having a dedicated line or cell phone for business purposes only could be essential.

Remember to keep all receipts for tax purposes; you may be able to use these expenditures as a tax write-off. Check with a tax accountant for specific details.

Funding your business

Because most stay-at-home mothers will be in business for themselves, as opposed to having employees, I don't recommend borrowing money from banks, relatives, or friends for start-up costs. The costs associated with bank loans usually make them cost-prohibitive for most home-based businesses.

In my opinion, it's better to start small and expand your business slowly as demand increases and income allows you to purchase needed equipment or supplies, instead of overextending yourself financially. That said, check the resource section at the end of this chapter for a list of books and websites that will provide information on acquiring a bank loan for your business, should you choose that route.

Many at-home jobs require no overhead or start-up expenses at all. Tonya Travelstead, who teaches piano and sells books and collectibles online, does not have any overhead expenses associated with her businesses. "Besides not needing a business wardrobe, I also do not need to meet clients at an office or at restaurants, thus saving those expenses as well," says the Maitland, Florida, mother of two teenagers.

I also strongly oppose tapping your home equity through either lines of credit or loans for seed money. In addition to the costs associated with such loans or credit lines, if your business should fail and you cannot repay the loan, you could lose your house. So where will you find your start-up funds? Here are a few suggestions:

Save. Yep, that's right. I highly recommend reducing your spending and setting aside every spare penny to get your business off the ground. (Re-read chapter 3 for information on spending plans or budgeting.)

Review your list of necessities for starting your business and see if you can either do without or downgrade, at least in the beginning. For instance, you might want a high-speed Internet connection but perhaps you could manage with dial-up service in the initial stage. Or maybe you could stop by your local public library to use their Internet connection if you need a faster speed on occasion.

Once you have a rock-bottom list and cost analysis, start socking money away to meet that goal. With your husband's agreement, put every spare cent toward getting your business off the ground. As you save, use this time to work on your business plan, conduct extensive market research, develop your marketing strategies, and perfect your product or service.

Sell something. If your start-up costs are modest, you could raise the cash by downsizing your household goods. Hold a yard sale. Sell larger items, like furniture, through consignment stores, online websites like *www.CraigsList.org*, or newspaper classifieds. (Many major newspapers, such as the *Washington Post*, now offer free classified ads for goods for sale under two hundred and fifty dollars.) You'll get a cleaner, less cluttered house, plus money for your business.

Use funds you already have. I'm not advocating raiding your retirement fund, IRA account, or college savings accounts. However, if your general savings account has more than six months' living expenses—and you have sufficient funds elsewhere for unexpected emergencies, such as car repairs—consider using some of that money to start your business. This method should be used only as a last resort, though. Saving and or selling items are much safer bets than taking money out of any kind of account.

Make investors of family or friends. If friends or relatives have extra cash and are willing to bankroll seed money, you could informally accept such an advance with the expectation that when you start running a profit, you would pay them back over a certain period of time. However, if your business should go under, they would simply be out their investment. It would be a good idea to draw up some sort of agreement stating when and how they would be repaid their "investment." This is more of an agreement between friends than a true investment opportunity. I don't recommend this method, as it could strain relationships if your business does not take off as expected.

Organizing your business

Staying organized is key to keeping your business running smoothly. You will need to develop a good system for tracking business-related expenses, such as mileage to and from clients, invoices and income, current and potential client lists, and marketing efforts.

Your system does not have to be elaborate—just big enough for your needs. For example, you can keep all of your business-related expenses in a large envelope, file folder, or desk drawer. Use folders or an electronic spreadsheet program like Microsoft Excel to organize client names and numbers. For invoices, devise a simple numbering system and place them in one location, such as an electronic file folder. Money-management software, such as QuickBooks and Quicken, also can track business expenses, invoices, and tax information.

I have a variety of clients for my freelance work, and I label each invoice with an abbreviation and number that includes part of the current year. Each year I start over with 01. If I am billing a trade association for the first invoice of 2007, my invoice would read: TA Invoice 0107 for a Feature Story. When I receive payment, I staple the check stub to an invoice copy. I also record each invoice and amount on a master list, which makes it easy to access for tax purposes.

"We try to keep to a good budget so that our business does not hurt the family, but rather helps the family," says Beth McCord, who works from her home in Normal, Illinois, in direct sales for a company that offers nutritional supplements and skin care products. "We also tithe off of what we make and give thanks for all God does in our business. You need to see it as a business and treat it like a business no matter how many hours you set aside for it. If we treat it like a hobby, then it will take all our resources, money, energy, emotions, and time. A person who owns a store would not play around with his business. He must make sure he does well for his customer and his store. We need to think in the same respect and know that God called us to work hard unto him. Work is good."

Cash, check, or charge

Accepting payment from clients can be a sticky situation, given the prevalence of using plastic to pay for even items costing a dollar. Credit- and debit-card transactions carry with them hidden fees for merchants that make them cost-prohibitive for some small businesses.

If you sell to the general population, you may prefer to run a strictly cash business. If you do decide to accept checks, be sure to get a phone number and driver's license number for verification purposes. Money orders also can be a safe way to accept payment. For online purchases, consider signing up with PayPal or other similar, vetted services. When in doubt about a company's reputation, check with the Better Business Bureau.

For freelancers, reputable companies pay for your services with a company check. Be leery of accepting cash from companies for freelance work, as you do not want to be paid "under the table." Keep careful records of any cash payments you do receive to report as income at tax time. 🏠

Melissa Jenkins
Grant Writer

Melissa Jenkins was pleasantly surprised when her boss provided her with the opportunity to work part-time from home after the birth of her first daughter. "She gave me the opportunity to change some of what I was doing and to shift the focus to the tasks easier to do from home," says Melissa, who lives in Harrisonburg, Virginia, with her husband and two girls, ages three and eight months. "Her willingness to do that for me helped me make the decision to work from home."

Melissa goes into the office two mornings a week, but the rest of the time she works from home writing grants and communication pieces for a children's organization. The company helped to set up her home office with an Internet connection and access to the company's computer network.

For the past two and a half years, she has been working about twenty hours a week at her job. "I feel that I am using my talents for the Lord," says Melissa.

Her husband helps out by watching the girls when she has to go into the office. "He has a flexible schedule, so we don't have to pay for childcare." Overall, her husband has been very supportive and understanding of her work. He even designs the newsletter for the group on the side. "He understands and supports the mission of the organization I work for and why I do what I'm doing," she says.

As with most Christian women, Melissa wrestles with her roles and responsibilities as a mother and as an employee. "I don't want to shortchange my husband or daughters, but I also enjoy work. My first responsibility is to be my girls' mother and my husband's wife as called by God, but I know, too, that I need to honor my employer by being honest about my time and actually producing results."

Along with that struggle, having two small children means she has less uninterrupted time to work. "It's harder to work during the daytime, so I need to do more in the evening, which sometimes compromises family time or time with my husband," says Melissa.

Time management, along with self-discipline, is key to her success at being a wife, mother, and employee. "It's a challenge with self-discipline, because I'm not particularly good at that," she admits. "Every day I struggle with time for family and time for work—working from home is one more thing to fit in at home with all the distractions of the housework, kids, and husband."

Doing things to suit her schedule is a big plus for Melissa. "I'm generally able to fit work into my schedule unless I have a pressing deadline." She enjoys going into the office two mornings a week because she can make uninterrupted phone calls, meet with other employees, and keep up with the work that everyone else is doing. But working at home enables her to work at her own pace and to set aside work to do things with her girls. "I wouldn't trade being home with my girls for any job, but being able to do both has been wonderful," she says. "It has really meant the world to me. My boss has given me an enormous gift by helping me to work from home."

While she sometime feels like she's alone in working from home, she's heartened to hear about other at-home women with employment. "Sometimes you wonder if you're being judged by other Christians because you are working," says Melissa. "Right now, this arrangement is working for me and my family, and I'm happy that I can work from home."

Sherry Lanier
Database Administrator

Sherry Lanier has found that her role as a Christian wife and mother has been enhanced by her at-home work as a database administrator for a seminary.

Ten years ago, Sherry started working from home when her daughter was a teenager, logging between fifteen and twenty hours per week. "With the type of work that I do—working off the Internet—if my husband is traveling for his job, I can travel with him because anywhere I go, I've got Internet access," she says. "The convenience and flexibility of my job also enabled me to homeschool our daughter."

Her husband loves her at-home work. "Whenever he has a break in the day, he will call me to meet for lunch. My job allows me to be flexible with his schedule so that we can do more things together," she explains, adding, "I'm a very active person, who likes to have my time directed, so this job gave me a way to be able to do that."

Because working from home tends to isolate her, Sherry works hard at engaging in relationships outside the home. "I go to lunch with other women fairly often. I also find I have more opportunities for ministry being at home. Currently I am mentoring some single women who come to my home for discipleship."

Sherry finds herself more focused and more productive working at home. "You don't have the office politics and don't have the travel or clothing expenses. Your other expenses are nominal as well. For me, it's a win-win situation. Your financial income goes further because you don't have these other expenses, plus your environment can be so pleasant. My at-home job has been a tremendous blessing and benefit to us."

She cautions other mothers, especially those with children still at home, to remember to keep a balance between work and home. "Don't let work overcome the time and need to focus on your children," she advises. "You still need to keep a balance of relationships outside the home with your peer group and still engage in church activities and other relationships."

Sherry recommends engaging in activities that you enjoy, such as participating in a mother's morning out program when your children are young. "While your children are in the program, make a lunch date with a friend or join a noon-day Bible study; if one is not available, consider starting one. If you enjoy tennis, set aside a few hours each week to play. If your church has a tutoring program, volunteer an hour each week to help. Let your passion and natural interests be your guide as you prayerfully consider the multitude of options available to you."

She adds, "Just be careful you're not just becoming so closed in to your family that you lose the big picture of the kingdom. Engage in culture outside the home both with and without your children."

Beth McCord
Direct Sales Representative

Beth McCord transitioned from a customer to a seller for a glyconutrient supplement company. "I am a stay-at-home mom of an eight-year-old and a six-year-old, and I do not want a job that takes me away from my family," she remarks. She had done other direct sales jobs before and enjoyed working her own hours. But once she took supplements for her fibromyalgia and psoriasis, and got completely well, she felt called to share this information with others to help them with their health issues. "I feel as though I work for the best company. The company is number five on the Forbes Top 200 Small Companies and is truly seeking to glorify God in all they do with these incredible products," she says.

For the past two years, Beth has sold the products from her Normal, Illinois, home, working between fifteen and twenty-five hours a week. As a pastor's wife, she separates her work clients from the church congregation as much as possible. "We feel strongly that I must keep relationships first and foremost, and not my business, when it comes to those in our congregation. God has taught me to be patient and wait on him. We never want others to feel obligated to buy or join the business side, and we leave this up to God." She now has three people who have joined her organization of their own accord, "with no pressure or persuasion," she says. "I have about six people on the supplements that have seen incredible improvements and they tell others to talk with me. This opens doors without me banging down the doors."

Her husband is her number-one supporter and balancer. "He cheers me on, helps me to have meetings by watching the kids and makes sure I have time to get my work done. He also keeps my heart in check. If he senses my heart is getting greedy or pushing forward too quickly (on my terms) then he gently restores me," says Beth. "He also helps me brainstorm ideas for making my business more successful. I am truly blessed to have a supportive husband."

Some disadvantages of the business for Beth are not knowing how much money she will make. She relies on others she supervises to help her business by building their own businesses. "The pay can change all the time and I need to help those I supervise to succeed as well as follow up with many customers to be sure they are satisfied. This can eat up a great deal of time, energy, and emotions. Some people do not like anything that is part of a network marketing venue, and therefore that makes it difficult emotionally as well as stressful at times. It is also hard to maintain tax information and overhead expenses," she says.

But the advantages help offset some of the disadvantages. Choosing her own hours and investing what she wants into the business make it an attractive fit for her family life. "If we are having a hard time as a family, then I can decide to focus on them more and less on the business until things get straightened out. I also can put more time into my business when our life allows. I can take my business wherever I go, as each person is a possible prospect, customer, or new associate. I can be working while at my kids' sporting events, grocery store, or doctor's office," says Beth.

"Also, it has been a huge support for my health. I need these supplements to remain well and not have the same major issues that I had struggled with for years." The McCords could not afford the supplements on her husband's salary, so her job with the company enables her to get free supplements as well as earn extra money.

Beth encourages other stay-at-home moms who want to work from home to "constantly check our heart motives to see if we are following God's lead or our own. We must realize that our job can be a ministry to others with whom we come in contact. Seek how the Lord would want you to use your business to glorify him and to bring others closer to him."

Tina Simpson
Missionary Recruiter

Since 1999, Tina Simpson has worked from home for the missionary arm of a Protestant denomination as a missionary recruiter, spending thirty hours a week talking with people interested in long-term and two-year mission service. "I talk regularly with hundreds of people. I develop relationships with them, talk through qualifications, help narrow down opportunities/fields, and coach them through the application process—or encourage them if they choose to pursue another line of service," says the Atlanta, Georgia-based mother of four children, ages seven, six, four, and one.

When pregnant with her first child, Tina assumed she would need to quit her full-time recruiter job. "I feel confident that I should be taking care of my own children—especially because my reason for working is not financial, but more for my own emotional well-being," she says. But her boss wanted her to stay on as a telecommuter, offering to set up her home office with all the things she needed to do her job from home. Because of her boss's actions, she decided to stay with the organization. Her husband fully supports her work-from-home arrangement, given that it fulfills their desire that she be at home with their children.

"I was thirty-six when I became a mom, partly having put it off because I loved my job and didn't know they'd let anyone work *virtually*," explains Tina. "I have a very, very strong work ethic, but also a love of missions and people because I grew up as a missionary kid in the Himalayas of India."

To squeeze in thirty hours each week, she usually works around the children's schedules during the week and also puts in long days on Saturdays. Two of her children are in school full time, with another in preschool three mornings a week. During school and nap time for her youngest, she schedules her work phone calls before noon or after eight at night during the week.

"I work an average of five hours a day, six days a week, most of which are done when the kids aren't home or are asleep. I'm a night owl, so it works well for me to be calling California at eleven-thirty in the evening Eastern Time. ... I've definitely perfected the art of multitasking." She does go into the office three Sunday evenings a year to meet her recruits in town for a retreat that her department sponsors.

Balance is her biggest challenge. "If anything, my family gets the raw end of the deal from time to time," she admits. "The 'problem' is that I love my job (as well as my children of course!) and I'm a very conscientious worker. If I were honest, I'd have to say that especially in the last year or two, I've felt a little guilty about not playing all afternoon and evening with my kids. I do love that they have playmates in each other, so they aren't bored, but I could probably be stimulating their minds more."

Tina creates adult social time for herself by meeting with other moms, and she finds that even her time spent talking to recruits on the phone fulfills a need for adult interaction.

Overall, Tina is happy with many aspects of her work-at-home job. "I love the flexibility, variety, ability to exhibit self-dis-cipline. I like not having to dress up and look 'professional' day after day, not having the Atlanta commute, not having so many meetings interrupt my workday," she says. "The organization has gone the extra mile to accommodate me. For example, it's not easy helping a 'remote' person twenty miles away from the office whose phone or computer aren't working. I really appre-ciate that, and the fact that I'm not expected to be at many of the meetings that would require finding a daytime babysitter."

Tonya Travelstead
Piano Teacher and Internet Collectibles Seller

Tonya Travelstead and her husband decided before they got married that when children came along, she would stay home with them. With two teenage sons whom Tonya homeschools, she knew any work would need to fit into her at-home sched-ule. With a background in music, she began teaching piano from her home ten years ago, but had to cut back on the num-ber of students when her oldest son began playing varsity bas-ketball. Two years ago, she added selling books and collectibles online at eBay, *Amazon.com*, and *Half.com*. Now she spends ten to twelve hours per week on both jobs from her home in Maitland, Florida.

"We feel that it's in the best interest of the family for the parents, rather than someone else with conflicting values, to nurture and train children while they are young. Being home with them has been perfect for this since teachable moments occur often outside of the homeschooling instruction," she says.

Tonya structures her day around her homeschooling, work-ing early in the morning on the Internet sales and teaching piano in the afternoons. She tries to limit herself to a few hours of work per day because "I'm very project-oriented, so I like to continue until everything is done. As a mom at home, it's mostly piecemeal, a little at a time.

"There's always something to do for the home when you

are at home and it's always staring you in the face. I have to prioritize chores to fit everything in that needs to be done each day—cooking, cleaning, laundry, bill paying. The children are old enough to help with everything, though, and that helps me."

She takes pleasure in the fact that her children can come and talk with her whenever they need to, "although sometimes I have to say flatly that I need this hour or two to finish something." Tonya also has more time available for church ministry. The family uses the extra money she generates for movies, dinners out, and sometimes even vacations or short trips—all without straining the family budget.

"You can be as creative as you want to be and do what you enjoy while contributing to the family income pool," she says about working from home.

Resources
Books

The Complete Idiot's Guide to Starting a Home-Based Business
by Barbara Weltman

How to Fund Your Business: The Essential Guide to Raising Finance to Start And Grow Your Business
by Steve Parks

Working for Yourself: An Entrepreneur's Guide to the Basics
by Jonathan Reuvid

Working for Yourself: Law & Taxes for Independent Contractors, Freelancers & Consultants
by Stephen Fishman

Online

Better Business Bureau
www.bbb.org
Provides information on the reliability of companies.

Inc. Magazine
www.inc.com
Provides information, products, online tools, and services for small business owners.

PayPal
www.paypal.com
Offers merchants of all sizes the ability to accept credit- and debit-card payments.

SCORE
800-634-0245
www.score.org
Provides a host of resources for small businesses, including access to a variety of experts.

Lawyers and Zoning and Taxes, Oh My!

The legal issues with your business

L egal issues can be an intimidating yet necessary component of any at-home business. Even if you are a freelance worker, you need to be aware of zoning laws, certification requirements, taxes, licenses, contracts, and insurance, to name a few.

Zoning laws

If customers come to your house on a regular basis for consultation, instruction, or to purchase goods, you may need special zoning permits.

Don't set up your home business without first checking with your city or county zoning department. While the officials might not notice your business, you can certainly bet your neighbors will. It's best to make sure you will be in compliance with zoning laws before opening for business.

Follow these general guidelines when setting up a home-based business, but check with the local zoning authority for any specific requirements.

■ Only members of your family living at that address may be involved in the business. This means that your sister who lives across town can not be involved in the business on a daily basis, but that your mother who resides permanently with you can be a part of the venture. You could have a partner that doesn't live with you, as long as they don't come to your house on a daily basis to work.

■ Using your home as a business should be subordinate to its residential use. In other words, your house is a home first—a business location second.

■ Each area has its own specific ordinances, but don't be surprised if you cannot change the outside appearance of your home other than adding a small, non-illuminated, flat-mounted sign no larger than one square foot. Some cities prohibit any type of business to be conducted in a residential zone.

■ Accessory buildings, such as garages, also can be regulated if used as a business. Which means you have to follow local zoning laws.

■ No large uptick in traffic volume associated with your home-based business is allowed. For instance, you cannot have lots of vehicles coming and going to your home on a regular basis.

■ Many ordinances also restrict the use and parking of commercial vehicles, such as delivery vans, on your property.

■ Equipment for your home-based business cannot create electrical interference, fumes, glare, noise, or vibration that can be detected off the property by the normal senses. For example, you cannot use equipment that your next-door neighbor can hear, smell, or feel clearly anywhere in their house.

■ You cannot keep inventory at your house other than products you have created or produced on-site. For example, storing lots of product in boxes in your basement would probably be in violation of this rule. Small amounts of direct-sales product are generally acceptable. However, check with the zoning office for specifics, as each city and county will have different definitions of inventory and acceptable limits.

■ Use of utilities or community facilities beyond normal residential use is prohibited.

■ If your business opens early in the morning or closes late at night, you might want to consider talking with your neighbors beforehand to explain the nature of your business and its customers.

Keep in mind that the main goal of zoning laws is to keep high volume or high traffic activities out of residential areas.

Certification requirements

Before hanging out your shingle, make sure you have the right certifications to operate your at-home business. For instance, if you will be selling homemade food items out of your home, such as for catering events, check with the local health department to find out if you need food-safety certification. Other professions, such as those in health care and education, also may require state certification. Some certifications require completion of state-sponsored or recognized courses, which will cost money to take.

Contact your state government under the department relating to your field, such as health or education, to see what, if any, certifications are necessary. Remember, too, that licenses or certifications need to be kept up-to-date. Plan accordingly to make sure you stay in compliance.

Trademark terminology

Depending on the success and scope of your business, you might want to consider protecting the name of the business or product formally by registering it with the U.S. Patent and Trademark Office (*www.uspto.gov*). Here are the different types of protection that exist:

Trademark. This registration applies to any word, name, symbol, device, or any combination used or intended to be used in commerce to identify and distinguish the goods of one manufacturer or seller from goods that are manufactured or sold by others; in short, a brand name. Examples include 7-Eleven®, SNICKERS®, and Coke®.

Service Mark. This registration applies to any word, name, symbol, device, or any combination used or intended to be used in commerce to identify and distinguish the services of one provider, from services provided by others and to indicate the source of the services. Examples include Wal-Mart℠, McDonald's℠, and AT&T℠.

Copyright. This registration applies to any literary, musical, choreographic, pictorial, graphic, audiovisual works, and, on rare occasions, recipes.

Business licenses

Most localities call for any business—whether retail, virtual, or home-based—to have a business license. Even freelancers need a license. I have a business license through the city of Fairfax, Virginia, for my freelance writing and editing business. Start with the city or county tax or treasurer's office to find the right department that licenses businesses.

For sole proprietorships, filling out a business license basically involves your name, Social Security number, address of business (home), and designation or type of business.

You usually will pay a one-time registration fee for the license. To renew each year, you pay a percentage of the amount you file with the Internal Revenue Service as taxable income relating to your business. Many localities only garner a percentage of your income over a certain amount. For instance, Fairfax City assesses my freelance work over an actual annual income of ten thousand dollars.

Since city or county officials have access to your state and federal tax returns, it's advisable to obtain a business license and to keep it up to date.

Client contracts

Contracts can be tricky. The more complicated the contracts—and the more money that is concerned—the more likely you will want to have an attorney take a look at them. However, if your business requires simple contracts, you might not need an attorney to get involved.

A good rule of thumb for needing a contract is if you think a verbal agreement would not suffice.

For example, if you want to do a big project for a new client that would require you to pay for a lot of initial expenses or put in a lot of time, a contract outlining the project and payment schedule would be wise.

For services like piano lessons or tutoring, requiring upfront payments might negate the need for a formal contract. The main purpose of a contract is to ensure you have legal recourse if the customer or client does not pay for the product or service rendered.

There are numerous websites devoted to providing free, legal contracts of all kinds: buying, selling, real estate, retail, etc. Check out the LawDepot (*www.lawdepot.com/contracts*) or www.1StepLegal.com for a plethora of contracts and other legal forms. Even the Microsoft Office Templates website (*http://office.microsoft. com/en-us/templates/default.aspx*) has some downloadable contracts. However, make sure that the forms comply with state law. Most sites offer state-specific forms, too.

Insurance

Having sufficient insurance is essential for your home-based business. While your business may be covered by existing insurance coverage, do not assume that is the case. (Not everyone who works at home requires additional insurance. Check with a qualified independent insurance agent to find out if your business needs business insurance coverage.)

The Independent Insurance Agents & Brokers of America (*www.iiaba.net*) offers the following tips to protect your home-based business:

■ Check your homeowners policy for coverage options. While homeowners insurance covers a limited amount of certain businesses items, most offer no liability insurance for home-based businesses.

■ Also not covered in many homeowners insurance policies is a business-interruption clause, which means there is no protection if a loss causes a home-based business to stop operating. However, a home-based business owner may be able to add an endorsement of this coverage to an existing homeowners policy. (An endorsement is a provision that is added to an existing insurance policy to modify its coverage; it's also called a rider.)

■ Research business-insurance policy options. Home-based businesses have several insurance options, such as incidental business endorsement, a business owners' package policy, or an in-home business owners' policy.

■ An endorsement on your homeowners policy can protect your business equipment, for example. Some insurance companies now offer riders that include property and limited business liability coverage, typically available to businesses generating five thousand dollars or less per year in receipts.

■ In-home business insurance provides protection for your business property, including general liability coverage. A business owners' package policy covers business property and equipment, loss of income and extra expenses, and liability—all on a much broader scale than an in-home business insurance policy.

Also check to be sure you have adequate insurance for yourself, especially if your home-based business is a full-time occupation. Consider adding or upping coverage for life insurance, health insurance, disability protection, and workers' compensation.

Collecting sales tax

If you sell items or services (like dog grooming or massages), you might be obligated to collect sales tax. Remember, even if you only sell items at a few arts-and-crafts festivals, you may be required to collect sales tax.

Because each state has different laws regarding what items or services need to be taxed—and who needs to collect that tax—consult a local tax accountant or your state's tax department for clarification. Doing this before you sell your first product can help you avoid owing back taxes.

Paying Uncle Sam

Like jobs outside the home, home-based businesses—including those who work from home as freelancers—must pay federal and state taxes. But don't let this section scare you. Understanding what you will owe and how to pay it is not too difficult, and it can save you hassles and headaches later.

The Internal Revenue Service (IRS) defines self-employed as being "in business for yourself, or carrying on a trade or business as a sole proprietor or an independent contractor. You are an independent contractor if the person for whom you perform services has only the right to control or direct the result of your work, not what will be done or how it will be done."[20]

For IRS purposes, your Social Security number or individual taxpayer number is your taxpayer identification number for your business. You will use this number when filing taxes.

If you are the least bit unsure about how to file when working from home, consult a tax accountant. It's worth the approximately three to five hundred dollars for peace of mind. However, you might want to do your taxes beforehand and then see what business-related deductions the accountant found. Compare the two returns to see what you missed. If the returns were close or exactly alike, you might not need to use an accountant every year.

"I have a certified public accountant do my taxes once a year," says Betty Pellissier, a Morgan City, Louisiana-based mom who manages one hundred and fifty bubble-gum vending machines. "I have a lot of write-offs, since I drive around servicing the machines."

Computer programs like TurboTax and TaxCut walk you through all the home-based business questions and deduction possibilities, and help with tax preparation for a fraction of the cost of an accountant. The IRS website (*www.irs.gov*) has an abundance of good information on self-employment and home-based businesses, including which forms you need and explanations of possible deductions.

If you work exclusively at home for one particular company (i.e., on the company payroll, not as a freelance worker), you might want to get a letter from that business stating that you work from home for the convenience of the company and that working from home is a condition of employment. This will help you avoid paying unnecessary or higher taxes, such as being taxed at a different rate or being assessed additional Social Security or other employment-related taxes an employer generally pays.

"I bill my own hours, so it is important that I use my time wisely and not waste taxpayer money," says Melissa Gindlesperger, who does data entry for a school system in Dacula, Georgia, which receives federal substance abuse prevention funding.

For home office deductions, you must use an area of your home regularly and exclusively for business purposes. Also, you must use the space as your principal place for a business that generates income. Recent law changes extend this requirement to those who perform administrative and managerial functions in a home office if they have no other fixed principal place of business; salespeople often fit in this category. Other ways to designate a home office is to use the space to meet clients, patients or customers, or use the area exclusively to keep business inventory or product samples.

When taking qualified business expense deductions, file IRS Form 8829: Expenses for Business Use of Your Home. Home-based business write-offs include one hundred percent of any expense directly related to the home office space, such as painting, cleaning, and even the premium for the home office endorsement on your homeowners insurance policy.

Other deductions include the cost of separate lines for telephone, fax, or Internet connections for your business. In addition, you can deduct a percentage of the indirect expenses related to your entire home, including mortgage interest, property taxes, rent, utilities, association fees, security monitoring, and general maintenance and repairs. To find this percentage, figure out the square footage of your home office space and then compute the percentage of your home's total square footage that it occupies. For instance, if your home has two thousand square feet of living space and your home office space is two hundred square feet, your office takes up ten percent of your home. Therefore, you can deduct ten percent of the utilities, rent, mortgage interest, and so on, for the year as related to your home-based business.

"I expense some items which enhance life, but are related to my home-based business of sewing window treatments, such as a cell phone, nice window treatments at home (my samples), gasoline reimbursement, computer, and my sewing machine," says Carolyn Wayland, a Richmond, Virginia, mom, with a teenage daughter. "And almost everywhere I go, I can sew something for someone and expense much of that trip."

Take photographs or a video to document that your home office space is used exclusively for your at-home work. You will need to keep copies of all business-related expenses throughout the year, including mileage and receipts for supplies. Storing them in one location will make tax time easier. Consult a tax accountant for clarification.

Another important tax-related item is paying quarterly state and federal taxes. This helps you avoid making a big tax payment when filing your taxes and can keep you out of trouble with the IRS.

A good rule of thumb is to pay at least ninety percent of the previous year's taxes in four installments for both federal and state government. The quarterly payments are due April 15 (first quarter), June 15 (second quarter), September 15 (third quarter), and January 15 (fourth quarter).

For example, say you owed two thousand dollars in income taxes related to your at-home work in 2006. In 2007, you would need to pay at least eighteen hundred dollars in taxes, or four payments of four hundred and fifty dollars, regardless of how much money you are making that year. Some accountants recommend paying the entire amount in one lump sum in the fourth quarter, while others say you must pay it in installments. Check with the IRS for clarification.

Once you start paying quarterly taxes, the IRS and state tax department will send you coupons to make payments. Programs like TurboTax also print federal and state quarterly estimate coupons after you file your taxes; a tax accountant likely will do the same.

Taxes for home-based businesses do not have to be scary if you keep careful records of all business-related expenditures and income, set up a quarterly payment schedule, and use a reliable filing program or accountant.

Melissa Gindlesperger
Data Entry Worker

When a former colleague contacted Melissa Gindlesperger to see if she wanted a job entering data from her home computer, the Dacula, Georgia, mom thought it would fit nicely into her schedule. Two years later, she still enjoys her two to four hours per month of at-home work, which provides additional money for birthdays and holidays for her three-year-old and ten-month-old sons.

Before having children, Melissa worked for the state of Georgia as a caseworker for its family and children services department, and then managed the state's federal substance abuse funding for Georgia's substance abuse department. Her at-home job uses some of the skills she acquired at those jobs, as she enters data for a school system that receives federal substance abuse prevention funding through the state via the regional system.

"The data input is a required part of the school system's contract with the state," says Melissa. "My former colleague asked me if I would enter her data, seeing as I was familiar with the forms and data from when she used to turn her data into me. This frees her up to do the actual work."

Melissa also is an independent adoption agent, which means she is available to provide assessments to the county superior court for families seeking to adopt. "I have been called upon once to provide such an assessment," she says.

Her husband has been very supportive of her work. Melissa says, "He's aware that I need to block out time to enter data. With one child, I worked during afternoon naptime. But when I had another child, I realized that I needed 'naptime' as well and began working after the children were in bed at night."

One of the challenges Melissa faces is motivation. "It's hard to get on the computer and work after all my mom duties are completed for the day. But I love the flexibility of no time clock to punch and that I can schedule the work when I am available."

However, she wishes that other people would not assume that all she does are her "mom" duties at home, since she doesn't leave the house for her data entry job. "Working from home still has some image issues—such as folks thinking that you are stuffing envelopes," says Melissa.

"I used contacts from my previous employment to get my at-home job. I do what I used to do, I just do it from a different angle and at home. Other moms need to look within their own circles and experiences to find at-home work."

She also wants the church to realize that moms are changing, with fewer moms in local churches who solely stay at home with no other duties.

"We have work-from-home moms, moms who homeschool their kids, moms who care for aging parents, etc. Our church leaders need to get to know their women, and the best ways to serve them and allow them to serve the body. Traditional methods aren't going to work with today's mom."

Betty Pellissier
Vending Machine Owner

Betty Pellissier started her business eight years ago by buying thirty-five vending machines. With two grown children, she wanted a job that wouldn't take too much of her time. The Morgan City, Louisiana-based mom now has a hundred and fifty machines that she has placed at businesses, such as beauty shops, bank lobbies, tire stores, and hotels.

She services them once a month, working about twenty-five to thirty hours total. "These machines are the ones you see with bubble gum in them for twenty-five cents," she says. "They are so easy to carry and to service—this is a great job for a woman."

Her next-door neighbor started buying vending machines, too, and now the two of them do their rounds together, since their routes overlap. "She will buy my business when I retire in five years, so I'm training her now," adds Betty.

The machines quickly paid for themselves and Betty says she makes a tidy profit on them each year. "I just think I have a great job!" she says.

Carolyn Wayland
Seamstress

Carolyn Wayland does more than sew window treatments for customers—she also prays for each customer as she sews their order. "I can share the Gospel with my customers without worrying that I'll offend anyone," says the Midlothian, Virginia, mom.

She started her at-home sewing business four years ago when her daughter was still in high school. Now, she spends twenty-five hours per week sewing and even has a partner who sews slipcovers when Carolyn finds work for her. "She gives me a commission," she says.

When thinking about at-home work, she wanted something that provided a good hourly rate and the flexibility to fit into her homeschooling schedule. "Even though I have a master's degree in another field, sewing has been a great 'fit' for our family," she says.

Although her husband is not "thrilled" about the dining room always being covered in fabric, "he is extremely thankful for the income; that I'm still a homemaker most of the time; that I'm available for him and our daughter; and that there is activity in the house so the dog isn't lonely," says Carolyn. "My husband thinks it might be too stressful if I had to work elsewhere. We don't want that disruption and distraction for our family."

Carolyn schedules her sewing to fit into her daily activities. "I still go to my weekly Bible study. I grocery shop, etc." she says. She finds the schedule, money, and the satisfaction of seeing projects completed as some advantages to working from home. She also enjoys knowing she can turn down work whenever she must.

"The greatest part of this adventure has been trusting the Lord to provide the work. I never know what new job will appear when I'm finishing one, and sometimes the Lord gives me time off to catch up on neglected housework. But his provision has been amazing," says Carolyn.

She sees her sewing business as one that anyone could do. "The women who have been sewing for a long time—like quilters of old—are generally sweet, very generous, and helpful with one another, sharing patterns, techniques, and encouragement. Plus there are a million windows out there, so there's no threat of a shortage of work. Last year my profit income quadrupled—very nice!"

Meagan Price
Communications Consultant

When Meagan Price's husband enrolled in an out-of-state seminary in 2003, she asked her supervisors at the corporate headquarters of a major hotel chain if she could work remotely since they would be moving. "I needed to continue to work to support us," she explains. "They agreed to a three-month trial, after which all parties agreed the arrangement was working well and it should continue."

At the beginning of the arrangement, Meagan worked full-time from home at her job as senior communications manager for the company's internal communications department. After her daughter was born two years ago, she continued her full-time status, with her mother-in-law providing childcare. Eighteen months after the birth of her daughter, Meagan scaled back her hours and joined the company's temporary staff as a communications consultant. Now living in Pittsburgh, Pennsylvania, she works between three and fifteen hours a week, and is able to care for her two-year-old daughter and newborn son.

Not being in the office allowed her to distance herself from the office gossip, a plus for her. "Because I wasn't in the office, co-workers had to specifically call me to discuss work, which often didn't allow for a lot of chit-chat. That meant I wasn't privy to a lot of the rumors going around about people, and so wasn't tempted to hear or repeat things about co-workers."

Her work-from-home arrangement allowed her husband to attend graduate school full time, as well as providing the flexibility to spend more time as husband and wife, and for Meagan to spend more time with their children. When working full time at home, she arranged with her company to work normal business hours, but that sometimes bled into her home life.

"Before working from home, I typically left work at the office, rarely checking email or voice mail from home. However, once I started working from home, I checked email and voice mail at all hours of the day and into the night," she says. "I was much more accessible for my bosses. They knew I checked email at all hours, so they consequently expected me to respond at all hours."

Seeming to be available around the clock also proved to be an advantage because Meagan became the "go-to girl in my department for crisis communications. Even though I was out-of-sight, I was never out-of-mind. In fact, I was the first person my bosses often thought of to get the most critical communications out."

With more pressures on her to perform in her job, she has a hard time not letting the lines between work and home life become fuzzy. "The biggest challenge is separating my time effectively between work-life and home-life. Oftentimes, I feel like I work from the time I wake up until the time I go to bed. I personally don't get a lot of downtime when trying to squeeze work in between baby naps and *Sesame Street*," says Meagan.

She found she did miss some of the interaction with her co-workers, which meant when she did come back to the office for the occasional meeting, she had to re-connect with people all over again. "I sometimes felt like those I didn't work with forgot I was even around. This was particularly true with some senior-level managers within my communications group who often seemed surprised to see me when I came to the office for a meeting."

By working at home, Meagan discovered she became much more productive. "I became much more focused on my work, allowing me to produce better quality work," she says. "I wasn't distracted by co-workers in the next cube or people stopping by my office to say hello. I could work more efficiently and effectively because I had nothing else taking my time or my attention. Consequently, about a year into my full-time work-from-home arrangement, I was given a promotion."

The flexibility allowed her to take short breaks while pregnant with her first child and still get her work done. "This proved especially helpful in two instances before and after I had my daughter. When I was pregnant with her, I struggled for many, many weeks with nausea. If my meeting schedule allowed, I would take a short nap in the afternoon when I felt the worst and then finish up my work after dinner when I felt the best of the day. Then, once I had my daughter, I was able to continue to breast-feed her at her scheduled times through-out the day. And I didn't have to worry about pumping milk at the office and the challenges that can entail."

For the mother who works from home, Meagan emphasizes the importance of maintaining a work and home balance. "It's tempting to think that just because you work from home, you have unlimited time to get your work done, make every meal a home cooked one, clean your house and care for your kids. But, balance is still extremely important, and it's difficult to maintain it effectively," she says.

Resources
Online

1st Step Legal
www.1steplegal.com
Provides links to legal forms and answers legal questions.

Independent Insurance Agents & Brokers of America
127 S. Peyton Street
Alexandria, VA 22314
800-221-7917
www.iiaba.net
Offers information on all types of insurance.

Internal Revenue Service
www.irs.gov/businesses
Provides downloadable forms and tax information for small businesses.

LawDepot.com
www.lawdepot.com
Provides a plethora of downloadable legal and business-related forms.

Microsoft Office Online
http://office.microsoft.com/en-us/templates/default.aspx
Offers many templates relating to business needs, such as budgets, contracts, and expense reports.

TaxCut
www.taxcut.com
From H&R Block; provides software for filing federal and state taxes.

TurboTax
www.turbotax.intuit.com
Provides income tax filing software for both federal and state, including one for businesses.

U.S. Patent and Trademark Office
800-786-9199
571-272-1000
www.uspto.gov
Provides information on how to trademark your business name.

10

Time for Your Debut

How to market your business

Marketing your business, service, or products can be as simple as putting up flyers at local businesses or as elaborate as a direct-mail campaign. With the Internet and email, you can advertise your business to virtually anyone in the world for a relatively low cost. Developing an effective marketing plan can boost business and improve your bottom line.

Everything you do to promote your business is considered marketing—handing out flyers, giving presentations, advertising, signage, direct-mail pieces, press releases, brochures, business cards, email, and websites.

To be most effective in reaching your target audience, and to give a good return on your marketing dollars, put together a comprehensive marketing plan. This plan, like your business, should start small and grow to reach more potential customers as you expand.

Creating a marketing plan

First, revisit the research you pulled together on your target customer. Gather more details (if necessary) to develop the appropriate detailed profile of a typical client: age, gender, marital status, economic status, religious preference, location, and what need your business will fulfill. For example, if your business is being a personal chef, your typical client might be a married, working mother who lives within a ten-mile radius of your home. If you also want to offer kosher meals, then you could add "observant Jew" to your criteria.

Second, use that profile to write your marketing plan, using some of the marketing ideas mentioned later on in this chapter.

Third, create a website for your business.

Fourth, join a local business association or chamber of commerce for networking opportunities. These organizations also provide workshops and seminars for members that can provide information to help your business grow.

Take a look at this sample first year marketing plan for a personal chef business called Cooking For You. The slogan is: *Homecooked Meals Without the Hassle.*

■ Order 500 business cards.

■ Create website with sample menus, prices, and a form to request a follow-up call.

■ Donate a four-course dinner for two to the local elementary school auction and to the local anti-hunger organization's silent auction.

■ Print flyers to place in area grocery and specialty food stores (with permission).

■ Use captured emails from website and events to send out monthly "What's Cooking" newsletter.

Creating marketing materials

Once you outline the marketing plan, be sure to have the materials professionally designed and/or written. Nothing screams "She doesn't have a real business" louder than a poorly designed and mistake-riddled advertisement, brochure, mailing, or website.

If you don't have the skills to design or write a great brochure, consider hiring someone to do so. If you make the piece generic enough (i.e., no specific dates or items that would make the piece out of date in a month or two), such a brochure could last several years and be well-worth the money spent on its development. Also, you could barter with other moms or friends who have graphic design or writing skills to get a quality item. Even if you don't think your at-home business would be something worth a trade, perhaps a home-cooked meal, babysitting, or housecleaning help would be a welcome swap.

After your piece is designed, don't skimp on the printing quality. Call around to find out the best price for the highest quality paper and printing. You generally receive a better price for higher quantities (like for orders of a thousand or more), so ask about price breaks for a range of quantities.

When writing copy, short and simple is usually best. With all the distractions, most Americans have increasingly short attention spans, so less copy is better.

Think about a slogan or phrase to describe your service. Get input from family and friends. Really spend some time crafting a good, pithy description, but try not to be so clever that the phrase obscures the meaning of your business.

As you write, think about how your words could be illustrated to catch readers' attention. There are many websites that have low-cost and royalty-free photographs and illustrations available to enhance your marketing pieces; see the resource section at the end of the chapter for a list. For our community swimming pool's brochure to advertise its brand-new pool, I wrote the opening copy, "Splash Into Summer at the Brand-New Fairfax Swimming Pool," and added a great photograph of two girls jumping into a pool, for which I paid around six dollars at *Istockphoto.com.*

Don't forget to list several ways for your customers to contact you: website URL, telephone or cell phone number, email address, mailing address, and physical address (if you have clients that come to your house).

Bethany Giles, who worked from home as a freelance writer, found that she had to actively market herself to magazines before finding one client who gave her regular assignments. "I wrote on various subjects and had one client who was my mainstay throughout the year. Others came and went with their need for my services," says the Sheffield, Alabama-based mom of two children ages nine and four. By developing a marketing plan, Bethany was able to keep her workflow at a steady pace.

Once you have a good slogan and basic copy about your business ready to go, it's time to consider what marketing strategies to employ: high-cost, low-cost, and no-cost.

High-cost marketing ideas

Sometimes it pays to spend money on a splashy marketing campaign, if, for instance, you are launching a new product, expanding your business, or hosting an event.

Advertisements in newspapers and magazines can be expensive, but if you hit your target audience, they may be worth the price. Places to consider advertising include local newspapers (both online and print editions), telephone books, and city directories (online and print). Work with a professional to design a great ad in order to maximize your investment.

Mail a professionally designed and written brochure to a select mailing list. You can get addresses for specific neighborhoods or areas within a city or county through the local real estate assessment office, sometimes for free if you are a city or county resident. Other resources for mailing lists include trade associations, your Chamber of Commerce, or organizations related to your business. Some lists will cost money, while others may be free. Do some research to make sure you are getting the best list, as a good one can be the basis of your marketing efforts for years to come and well worth the investment.

Direct-mail pieces also can be an effective way to reach potential clients. A direct-mail piece encompasses materials such as letters, testimonials, response forms, return envelopes, subscription forms, or any ads and coupons for your business. Examples of direct mail include magazine renewal notices, candidate mailings, non-profit donor solicitations, and coupon mailers.

Again, have your piece professionally produced. You can either mail the material yourself or piggyback it with other ads in mailers. If your business or service has a natural fit with another company of similar yet different services, ask about doing a mailing together to share costs. For example, if you're setting up a pet-sitting service, consider asking a nearby pet grooming salon to go together with you to target the same clientele with information on different products and services.

When Deborah Tate, a legal transcriptionist in Greenacres, Florida, decided to work at home she did a very simple direct-mail campaign. "I opened the phone book and found all the area court reporting agencies. I then typed an introductory letter about my at-home business and sent it to twenty agencies.

"My 'bait' was to offer to type for free a fifteen-minute tape so the prospective client could see my work at no risk. I waited four days after mailing the letters before calling each office to make sure they received the letter and to see if anyone went for the bait. Out of twenty letters, one court reporter responded positively.

"That was the beginning of my business."

Participate in local events that offer tables or booths for businesses, such as local festivals, fairs, children's events, and arts-and-crafts events. The cost for a booth can be all over the map, depending on the size of the event and expected attendance. Check your city or county website, visitor's bureau, or Chamber of Commerce for a list of indoor and outdoor events. Start at a smaller, less expensive event, and, as interest in your products grows, expand to larger ones.

Low-cost alternatives

Keeping your marketing budget small does not mean you will have limited options. Low-cost ways to promote your business abound.

Business cards are inexpensive, so you can have snazzy cards for a small outlay. Keep the cards clean and simple so potential clients can clearly read the pertinent information: name of business, your name (if different from business), mailing address, physical address (if applicable), telephone number, cell phone number (if you want to receive business calls on your mobile phone), fax number, email address, and website URL. Avoid too many graphics or clip art, which can detract from the card's purpose. If you have a slogan, include that as well. Many websites such as *www.VistaPrint.com* offer simple business card templates to help you design your own cards.

A well-designed flyer or leaflet can grab attention and will cost you a fraction of the price of a brochure or a direct-mail piece. While you probably do not want to pay someone to write and design a flyer, at least ask a few people to proofread it to avoid having embarrassing spelling or grammatical errors.

Flyers can reach potential customers in many ways. Place them on community bulletin boards in grocery and drug stores, restaurants, schools, gyms, and churches. But remember to ask permission first. If your target audience is contained within a certain area, like a neighborhood, then hand-delivering flyers to people's houses can be effective.

However, you cannot put flyers in mailboxes, as only mail delivered by the U.S. Postal Service is allowed by law to be placed in mailboxes. Also, respect "No Solicitations" signs when posted on front doors.

Flyers also can be handed out at local events or stores, but, again, check with management first as some locations may have rules prohibiting such activity. If you cannot or do not have time to pass out flyers yourself, consider hiring reliable teenagers to help you out.

Cross-promotion with local businesses that have similar

products can be relatively inexpensive marketing as well. For example, you can ask florists or photographers to post your flyer, business card, or brochure to advertise your services as a wedding caterer. Talk to those businesses about other cross-promotion ideas, such as you providing a light snack gratis for a photographer's open house in exchange for including your brochure in his welcome packet and a copy of his guest list.

Give away something for free at local charity events, such as a four-course dinner for two if you're a personal chef, a personalized landscape plan, or draperies for the living room.

The costs are minimal and it's good free publicity for your business. Schools, churches, and other nonprofit organizations often need items for charity events and silent and live auctions, so your contribution would be most welcome. However, pick the event carefully in order to maximize your exposure to the right audience.

If your business is selling something that you either made or represent, consider hosting an open house event at your residence, local community center, or church, depending on space and parking constraints. Advertise with a postcard mailing to interested parties, such as family, friends, former colleagues, church members, neighbors, club members, and current clients.

Post flyers about the event in appropriate stores and other locations. A successful open house will have a limited time frame, and offer a specific reason for the event, such as new spring merchandise, fall clearance, or Christmas in July.

An open house should also have an artful and creative merchandise display; a possible discount to attendees, such as ten percent off their entire purchase; and plenty of helpers on hand to wait on customers. Capture email and mailing addresses for future events or mailings.

No-cost marketing tips

There are also some very effective marketing ideas that will cost you nothing except your time.

Send a press release about your company, service, or product to local newspapers and city magazines. Make sure you have something newsworthy to say, though, such as your participation in a charity event, or an event you will be hosting that's open to the public. When you are involved in another organization's events, make sure your name is mentioned in all publicity materials, including press releases.

Write free articles relating to your business for local newspapers, newsletters, magazines, and for online city, county, or state websites. For example, you might write an article about ways to keep a shaggy dog cool in the summer if you have a pet grooming service. Develop a good relationship with the editors of these periodicals, positioning yourself as an expert in your field. When reporters need a source on your particular topic, you will be the one they call—reaping free publicity for your business.

Follow up with new clients by sending a thank-you note expressing your appreciation of their business and asking for referrals. My hairdresser does a great job of this—she calls me every six weeks or so to see how I am doing and reminds me it's time for another haircut. She's always very friendly but to the point, so I don't feel like she's wasting my time. I certainly remember to make an appointment with her when I need a trim.

Offer to speak to groups for free about topics relating to your business. You might give horticulture tips on household plants if you're a landscaper, or you can demonstrate simple holiday crafts for children if you're an art teacher. Find the right groups by visiting city or county websites and looking in newspaper calendar event listings.

Jennifer Coffin, a potter from Fairfax, Virginia, participates in workshops relating to her craft. For her, however, it's sometimes difficult for her to attend, given that most workshops are scheduled for Saturday and Sunday. "This excludes me from doing a full workshop as a participant or as a presenter, because Sundays are for worship," she says.

Finally, enlist the help of family and friends to get the word out. Let them know you would appreciate if they could mention your new business to others. Never underestimate the power of word-of-mouth referrals.

Setting up a website

Setting up a website can be one of the best ways to market your business. While it can be a daunting task for the technically impaired, solutions exist to make it easier and less stressful.

There are many tools available to help you develop and host a website, such as *www.NetworkSolutions.com* and *www.Register.com*. These and other websites offer assistance in securing domain names (the website address), setting up the actual site, and providing email addresses. Most services are relatively low cost.

If you would prefer to have someone else set up your site, make sure you receive training on how to update it. Good websites do not cost a lot of money; you just need creativity. A good website delivers what it promises and is quickly accessed (stay away from large photos, graphics, and sound and video clips, as the download time can turn potential customers away). Your website should have company information prominently displayed (including contact details), stay up-to-date, and allow user interaction—the ability to fill out a form to receive additional information or send an email. Start with these basics and expand your site as your business grows.

The Internet also provides a way to sell your product to a larger audience. Decide whether you want to sell items through your own site, as opposed to *www.eBay.com* or *www.craigslist.org*, for example. E-commerce is a system used for conducting business transactions of buying and selling goods and services via the computer network. It can be a good addition to some home-based businesses, but having a secure site costs more money. E-commerce does not mean that you need the ability to accept credit cards, as some online payment companies, such as PayPal, have accounts available for small businesses. Your bank might even have the ability to process online payments for you. Consult with a website designer with e-commerce experience for more details.

Once your site is active, make sure you register key words

with online business directories and search engines, such as *www.findwhat.com*, *www.google.com*, *www.msn.com*, and *www.yahoo.com*. Adding a blogging section to your site also can generate interest from potential customers.

"I have always enjoyed computers and learned to use the Internet in the early days," says Jennifer Clauson, who sells used books on the Internet out of her home in Xenia, Ohio. "While searching a book site, I discovered that my husband's personal library, for which we had only paid a small amount for many of the books, was worth a significant amount of money. We decided to sign up on the website for a month or two just to sell his duplicates. We were very successful early on. My husband would mostly pick the books to sell, and I would do the computer and packing work."

Email marketing

Email can be a great tool for small businesses, but if you don't manage it wisely, it also can be a time waster. When setting up your business email account, add a professional signature to your outgoing messages. This should list your name, company name (if different), address, phone number, cell phone number, fax number, email address, and website URL.

For your website, look into creating a "blind" email address or email form that will redirect mail to your current email address and, hopefully, filter out spam. A web designer can do this for you if you need assistance. For example, your "blind" address could be *janesmith@yourwebsiteaddress.com*, which would forward messages to your "real" address at *janesmith@earthlink. net.* Use your blind email address on all marketing materials to help eliminate email spam.

Always ask current clients and potential customers for their email address, but make it clear that you will never sell it to a third party. Use the email addresses to build a client base and start sending out monthly e-newsletters, keeping them informed about what's happening in your business.

Keep the newsletter short and direct recipients to your website for more information. The newsletter doesn't have to have fancy graphics, just well-written text. As your list grows, you might consider adding a few graphic elements to jazz up the text, but start out simple. Include an opt-out function for those who wish to discontinue receiving the newsletter. Stay on top of removing those who ask, as there's nothing more irritating than continuing to receive emails from a business long after you have requested to be removed from their list.

Be creative with your use of email—it's a great and inexpensive marketing tool that can bring in big results. However, be careful not to overuse it. And remember that spelling and grammar are as important in an email message as in a printed marketing piece: Both are representing your business, and you want the best possible face to show customers.

Marketing your business can be a fun and rewarding experience, limited only by your creativity and energy. Start with the no- and low-cost options, and watch your business grow.

Jennifer Clauson
Internet Bookseller

"I believe women should be encouraged to evaluate their particular skills and think about what sort of business fits with their personality," says Jennifer Clauson, who sells children's, Christian, and scholarly books on the Internet from her home in Xenia, Ohio.

"I have seen too many ladies jump at multilevel marketing and home show businesses without looking around their communities and filling a need with their business. They need to realize that a home business takes time and is not always the solution for mothers with several young children. They need to have the confidence and support of their husbands. They need to be practical."

Jennifer started her Internet bookselling business, which she operated along with a bookstore, nine years ago with virtually no start-up costs. "My husband is a university professor who loves books, so we spent much of our leisure time in used bookstores and at library sales," she explains. "Our home was filling up with books, and our budget was suffering."

When her third child was an infant, things got "out of control" with the business. "I was so busy with the business, I was neglecting my children, husband, and housework. I was stressed and crabby all the time. At that point, we hired a full-time employee and I went back to being a full-time mom with a part-time business. Unfortunately, this made taxes and bookkeeping difficult. When my husband got a job teaching at an out-of-state university, we moved and sold our bookstore. Once we relocated, we decided to keep the business online and small enough to keep our sanity. We have done this well for five years."

Now that her four children, ages fourteen, twelve, nine, and six, are in school, Jennifer has more time to devote to the online business, spending between seven and twenty-five hours a week on it.

She tries to focus on selling books that enrich lives. "Sometimes it is a temptation to sell a high-priced book that is very contrary to our beliefs. I try not to, but sometimes they slip through without me noticing the content. This doesn't mean I don't sell books counter to my beliefs, but I try to make sure they would be useful for scholarship. For example, we sell copies of the Koran and Book of Mormon, because I know people, like my husband, use them in church history classes," she says.

Jennifer and her husband have weekly "dates," where they go book scouting and have dinner. "We also go on an out-of-town trip without the kids at least once a year to a huge book sale," she adds.

The convenience of an Internet business means she can do the work whenever she has time, which translates into whenever the children are at school or in bed. However, she does have trouble finding the time to keep her house clean with books "always gathering in piles where they shouldn't. It is a challenge for people to understand that though I have a flexible schedule, the work still has to get done. People always think to call me when they need someone's help during the day. That puts a lot of pressure on my schedule. We also have to sacrifice a good amount of space in our house for book storage."

Her work pulls at her because there's "always business work you could be doing and it can infringe on family time. And people sometimes call at inconvenient times. I also miss the daily interaction with adults that I would have if I worked in an office. Other stay-at-home moms satisfy this need by doing social hobbies or volunteering, but I just don't have time to do much outside of family and church activities."

Jennifer Coffin
Potter

"Creating pottery gives me purpose and an outlet for doing something I think is valuable and rewarding," says Jennifer Coffin, a potter from Fairfax, Virginia. "To bring the beauty of the natural materials given to us in creation into homes is important."

She loves pottery and working with her hands in the quiet of her own studio, which is in the basement of her home. There, she works anywhere between ten and thirty hours a week creating one-of-a-kind and functional stoneware.

She's been a potter for about thirty years, with breaks after each of her three children, now grown, were born. "I found that I could begin to work again when they were about two years old and could play on the other side of a gate where they could see me but could not get to what I was doing." she says. "I have been doing this for so long now it is hard for me to assess how it has changed my schedule. It is part of my life."

Because her husband has studied Christianity and the arts, he has a high view of the value that the arts play in the world and in their community of believers, she says, and he's very supportive of her work.

"We both believe that it's important for men and women to be productive members of their household. When the kids go off to school (if they do), you should not waste time on non-productive activities. Those times need to be scheduled but not indulged. Each woman has been given gifts more than just being a wife and mother. To find those gifts and develop them is valuable to the person and the family, and therefore to the community, both religious and secular."

Jennifer enjoys working at home, but responsibilities and ongoing projects can be a distraction from her pottery. "Making sure to work at the scheduled times is difficult because it is easy to find other things to do," she says.

She loves making her own schedule and having the opportunity to work at any given time. "Rather than facing a commute I can just walk into my studio to finish something up."

Another big plus to a home studio is not having the distraction of co-workers. "As an artist, it seems that I need time—extended time—to get to the place that other responsibilities recede into the background and my creativity comes forward," she says.

Bethany Giles
Freelance Journalist

For one year, Bethany Giles worked from home as a freelance journalist. The Sheffield, Alabama, mother of two children, ages nine and four, decided to try working from home after being a journalist for nineteen years earlier in her career. While at home she wrote for magazines and had one client who gave her regular assignments, spending between fifteen and thirty hours per week on her work.

Her decision to work from home was spurred by her daughter's severe eczema at age one, which flared up suddenly from contact with the chemical residue from cleaning products used at her daycare center. Bethany left a very low-stress job as a church secretary and administrator to write from home in order to keep her daughter at home.

While working from home, she worried about how to set priorities in order to fulfill her duties as a journalist, mom, wife, and church member. "Without daycare, my workday ended before three in the afternoon every day so I could pick up my son from school. With my daughter at home, my workday was interrupted numerous times with her needing a hug, snack, meal, diaper, etc. While it was a lot of fun to spend time with her, it was very difficult working with a toddler."

Bethany also found that people thought she had a lot of free time. "The school would call with requests for my time, my parents wanted to visit during the week, my husband had scads of errands for me to run and my church always had a need that I really wanted to fill that could only be done on a weekday. I also tried to keep all the household chores to the daytime hours, so we could enjoy our evenings as a family, but that cut into work time, too. I ended up working a lot in the middle of the night while everyone slept."

While she enjoyed setting her own hours around other activities, family trips, and holiday obligations, she eventually made the decision to go back to an office once her daughter was well enough for daycare again. "I went back to an office job because of insufficient income," she explains. "Freelance journalism was too irregular to depend on. Some months, I would have a paycheck every two weeks; other months, there would be one very small check and then a huge check the following month. Of course, the less I was able to work, the less money I could make. Time was always an issue."

Working from home did give Bethany more flexibility. "I really miss being able to take my work on the road with me for spring break or fall vacation. Now I am only able to go on one of my family's three annual trips, since I don't have the time available in my job."

She found it difficult to balance children, home, and work while also working from home, although she concedes it might have been easier if her children had both been in school. She also wonders how much time is okay to give to others out of her work. "Is it realistic to expect to earn a full-time salary while working at home and being a mom? Fathers certainly don't have the same expectations from others or problems of balance within their own minds that home-working moms do," says Bethany. "I guess I just want to do too much with my days."

Deborah Tate
Transcriptionist

When Deborah Tate was pregnant with her second child twenty years ago and working part-time at a law office, she decided to improve her skills and learn as much as possible about the law in order to begin an at-home legal transcription service for court reporters.

"My husband and I were convinced that the best way to nurture our children was for us to be the ones doing the nurturing," she says. "When our oldest child was about eighteen months old, I entered the workforce at the law office, but I missed my baby terribly. When we learned we were going to have a second child, my husband and I knew it was time for me to stay home and make it work somehow."

She contacted area court reporters, looking for work transcribing their tape-recorded legal work, such as depositions, trials, hearings, sworn statements, and police interrogations. "At the beginning, I only worked for one court reporter. Since she was part-time, I didn't have a lot of hours per week, maybe fifteen," says Deborah. "But it provided excellent on-the-job training. Because this reporter liked my work, I eventually built up to five reporters in about three years' time." She works an average of thirty to thirty-five hours per week—all while homeschooling their three children, two of whom are now grown.

Over the years, her husband has been an excellent source of financial support, encouragement, and hands-on practical help. "He has always been a very involved husband and father," she says.

With work and homeschooling duties, her daily schedule is in a constant state of flux. "In the early days, with a four-year-old and a newborn to care for, my hours were pretty hit-and-miss. I worked when I could, mindful of deadlines, and tried to sleep whenever I could. As the children got older, of course, I could devise a more manageable schedule. Twenty years later, I have a pre-teen, the only child left at home, and things are quite different," says Deborah.

Instead of working only in the afternoons, she usually starts her workday in the morning because she's an early riser. With an older homeschooled child who is very independent in her studies, Deborah finds time to work during the day, too.

Over the past four years, she transitioned her transcription work from legal to primarily medical transcriptions. "It was a huge challenge for me to get used to a twenty-four-hour turn-around on all medical work because I have no training and hold no certificates in medical transcription. Just like with legal transcription, in which I learned terms through study, I taught myself by studying medical dictionaries and a human anatomy atlas." She started doing medical transcriptions part-time to get used to the terminology, and now works for general surgeons, a pulmonologist, two endocrinologists, an ophthalmologist and five oncologists.

Especially in the early years of her business, she grappled with convincing people that she was running a business and could not just stop and talk with friends. "It took a long time to be taken seriously as a business owner, but that is no longer an issue."

She emphasizes that disadvantages to working from home are real. "Any woman who thinks she is going to have an idyllic life running a home business with children underfoot is in for a rude awakening," she says. "To be taken seriously as a business owner, I had to make sure I fulfilled my obligations to my clients. I had to move mountains in some cases in order to follow through on deadlines and commitments. Frankly, my clients didn't care what my personal schedule was like—they only cared about their work, which they entrusted to me. I had to deliver the goods, no matter what."

While she likes not needing an expensive wardrobe, Deborah makes an effort to be nicely dressed, even though no one sees her at work. "I did not want to fall into the trap of being a mousy, dowdy work-at-home mom, so I still wear a freshly ironed blouse with my jeans, and I almost always style my hair and wear make-up. I always spritz on perfume every morning. It's important to me to do that, and it does help my professional attitude."

Through her home-based business, her children have witnessed firsthand what it takes to be successful in business and they have developed an excellent work ethic. "I was home to teach my children the value of not only working hard, but looking the part. Prospective employers value a fresh-faced, friendly, polite, and nicely-groomed employee."

Deborah wants other moms to know that she runs a very successful home business without a college degree. "I'm just a high school graduate, but I've always had an insatiable appetite for learning. You don't need a college degree to operate a successful home business—just courage, determination, and a teachable spirit."

Sharon Hill
Environmental Engineer

Sharon Hill views her life as an at-home mother and environmental engineer who consults from home as "having my cake and eating it, too." She wanted to keep her ten-year-old daughter at home with her, yet use her skills in the professional world.

From her home in The Woodlands, Texas, she works between ten and twenty hours a week for a consulting firm providing services to industrial and manufacturing clients to assist with air quality regulation compliance.

Sharon has been consulting from home on and off for seven years, and has a supportive husband who encourages her to keep her hours low. "My work is always there," says Sharon. "It's challenging to have the self-discipline to switch gears from work to mom. It's also difficult to not over-commit myself to work projects."

She misses having help with computer problems, but the advantages of not having a commute and having fewer clothing purchases outweighs that inconvenience. "Also, I can participate in many activities, and plan my work around things that I enjoy doing," says Sharon.

Resources
Books

Building a Web Site for Dummies
by David A. Crowder

Do It Yourself Advertising and Promotion: How to Produce Great Ads, Brochures, Catalogs, Direct Mail, Web Sites, and More, Third Edition
by Fred E. Hahn

How to Use the Internet to Advertise, Promote and Market Your Business or Website with Little or No Money
by Bruce C. Brown

Maximum Marketing, Minimum Dollars: The Top 50 Ways to Grow Your Small Business
by Kim T. Gordon

The Perfect Sales Piece: A Complete Do-It-Yourself Guide to Creating Brochures, Catalogs, Fliers, and Pamphlets
by Robert W. Bly

The Ultimate Guide to Electronic Marketing for Small Business: Low-Cost/High Return Tools and Techniques that Really Work
by Tom Antion

Online

Direct Marketing Association
www.the-dma.org
Provides guidelines and news about direct marketing.

Fotosearch
www.fotosearch.com
Provides a plethora of royalty-free photographs and images.

Istockphoto
www.istockphoto.com
Provides a wide variety of royalty-free, high-quality, low-cost photographs for purchase.

JupiterImages
www.jupiterimages.com
Provides numerous royalty-free photographs.

Network Solutions
www.networksolutions.com
Provides assistance in setting up a website, from registering the domain name to hosting the Web pages.

Register.com
www.register.com
Provides help in starting a website, from registration to building the content.

U.S. Chamber of Commerce
1615 H Street, NW
Washington, DC 20062-2000
202-659-6000
800-638-6582
www.uschamber.com
Provides a searchable database of local chambers of commerce.

zapdata
800-590-0065
www.zapdata.com
Provides company profiles, industry reports, prospective customer lists, and customer-base analysis.

11

The Great Juggling Act

Finding time for family, work, and you

Now that you're on your way to establishing a home-based business, let's talk about how to juggle family and work. Finding the time—and energy—to work part-time or full time from home and keep up with children and all of your other duties can be a Herculean task. Let's talk about how to manage your time wisely in order to meet your family and work obligations—and still have your sanity at day's end.

Back to the basics

Running a home is akin to running a business. As women, we set the tone in our homes, both the overall attitude and the environment.

If we lose control of one or both, our homes can suffer from chaos. Working in an atmosphere of disorder can sap the energy from us that we need to accomplish our tasks and duties.

To manage your home and a home-based business takes organization and skill. Having a daily schedule, however loose, will help you to find the time to work from home and still keep up with your family obligations and housework.

To begin structuring your day, pull out the list you made of your typical week and organize it according to the day of the week. For example, your daily list might include the following: get dressed, do the breakfast dishes, feed the family pet, get the children dressed, make lunches, take the children to school and then pick them up, and make dinner. On Tuesdays, you may take your daughter to art class after school, and on Thursdays your son has soccer practice in the early evening. Lay out your entire week with all the known variables, including grocery shopping, laundry, kids' activities, volunteer or church events, other weekly errands, pet duties, and so on.

Plan your days as much as possible, at least at first until you get used to your at-home work routine. Put the list in a prominent place so you can reference it at a glance throughout the week. Post your schedule on the refrigerator or on the doors of the entertainment center.

On Sunday evening before bed, review the coming week's schedule. This will help you focus on what needs to be done and what can perhaps be postponed if you find you need extra time to work on a project. Then take a closer look at each item to see how it fits into the day and whether or not you can scale back or trim time from the task without sacrificing quality.

"I have a pretty organized system," says Toni Friese, a St. Cloud, Minnesota, consultant with a direct-sales company that sells home accessories. She developed her own system so that she could maximize the time her toddler napped for work-related tasks. "I have a binder where I keep a tab for each day of the week. For example, under Monday's tab, I can see this is what I need to accomplish that day. This way, I'm not spending half of his nap time figuring out and organizing what I'm doing. I just put my work items in my routine and schedule."

Lists and schedules might not appeal to you, but they can be invaluable tools for getting things done in a timely manner. Give it a try for a month to see how such a schedule could help you stay on track. After a month, step back and take a look at how everything went. How did you handle the unexpected? Could you actually do the work you needed to do in the time you had allotted? Make adjustments accordingly, remembering that your schedule will become more fluid as you and your family adjust to the new routine.

Starting your day

One of the first things a stay-at-home mother should do every morning is get completely dressed, including shoes and jewelry, and fix her hair and makeup—just as if going to work in an office building. While you might not put on stockings, high heels, and a power suit, you should still wear clean, matching clothes without stains, rips, or tears (the exception being, naturally, if you plan on cleaning, working in the yard, or performing an equally messy task). You cannot expect to act professionally if you are not dressed and ready to face the world.

Once dressed for the day, it's time to tackle some of the housework that comes with having a husband, children, and possibly pets. No matter how big or small your home is, take a few minutes—and it can be done in as little as five minutes here and there—each morning and evening to keep your home looking clean and uncluttered.

Doing the dishes right after breakfast and then making sure the evening meal is underway by defrosting meat can be a huge time saver. Having the children pick up the house before bedtime will help start the morning with less clutter, which, in turn, will provide fewer distractions to you.

If you need assistance on how to keep your house clutter-free and neat, check out the FlyLady, aka Marla Cilley, website at *www.FlyLady.net*, which provides a host of tips for getting motivated and keeping up with the endless housework.

Keep in mind that you might have to scale back your expectations for housework if you take on a part-time business. For instance, you might not have time to cook as elaborately each night as you are used to, or you might only mop the kitchen floor twice a month instead of weekly. Don't let perfectionist tendencies overwhelm you—keep a good perspective about chores and other household duties.

Gather 'round the table

Once you have written out a daily routine, it's time to schedule a family meeting. If your children are old enough to participate (a good rule of thumb would be school-age), then include them. If not, just sit down with your husband to talk about your new schedule.

One thing to remember: You should have been discussing this with your spouse all along, so nothing you say at this meeting should come as a complete surprise to him. Only the nitty-gritty how-tos of working from home should be talked about in this family meeting. If you don't have your husband's support prior to this meeting, you need to talk about that privately with him and postpone the family meeting until those issues are resolved.

Because you might have to commit to working during the afternoons or a few evenings, your new work-at-home arrangement will affect all family members in different ways. Your children might have to start riding the bus to school in the mornings instead of you driving them every day, freeing up time for you to get your work done before picking them up from school and taking them to after-school activities. Or you might ask your husband if he could change his work schedule to help with childcare so that you could have more time for your work.

At this meeting, outline your proposed home-based business and the ways it will impact the family. Chore allocations might be different since some of your daytime hours will be devoted to working. (Remember, it's never too early for children to contribute to the household. See the resources section at the end of this chapter for tips on age-appropriate chores for children.) Assign your children a few daily chores, such as keeping their room picked up, setting and clearing the table, clearing their breakfast dishes, or making their own lunch.

Another way to pare down the time it takes to do housework is to schedule particular chores on particular days: Wednesday for laundry, or Tuesdays and Saturdays for vacuuming. For instance, I host a women's Bible study at my home Wednesday mornings. Each Tuesday, I know I have to clean my house. On the weeks we don't meet due to breaks, I have noticed that the cleaning sometimes slides into the next week because I don't have a deadline. To keep on track, I simply pretend that we're meeting every Wednesday in order to get my house cleaned on a weekly basis. Scheduling chores will help keep you on track for getting the weekly cleaning done in a timely manner.

One way to stay focused is to physically separate your office and home space. "We designed an office out of a walk-in closet with a window, and that helps me to keep work life separated from home life," says Angie Dixon, a mother of nine-year-old twins who works part-time for the family glass business based in Clover, South Carolina. "I contain it in one spot so that when the family sees me in that area, they know I'm working and they will respect that time and space. If you're spread out all over the house, it can be confusing for children to know that you're at work."

Take advantage of time-saving ideas relating to cooking meals, too. Setting aside one day a month to cook and freeze a bunch of meals can be a huge time-saver. Also, there are many businesses that assist you in making many meals all at once, like Let's Dish (*www.LetsDish.com*) and Dinners Done Right (*www.DinnersDoneRight.com*). These businesses provide the ingredients and you assemble the main course meals on-site in their kitchens.

A bit of pre-planning can make the evening meal less stressful and time-consuming for you.

At your family meeting, solicit input from your children and husband. While it's important to listen to your children's concerns, you need to remember that you are the parent and that children don't like change.

While you should try to resolve any fears or concerns your children may have, as long as you have prayed about this opportunity—and you and your husband feel it would be beneficial to you and the family—you don't have to scrap the idea of moving forward just because working from home might make your kids uncomfortable.

Mommy the businessowner

If you have young children at home, or you homeschool your children, establishing guidelines while Mommy's working can be difficult, but not impossible. As I wrote this book, my four-year-old, two-year-old, and six-month-old children would frequently play nearby.

Sometimes I have frequent interruptions because they don't always understand when Mommy has to take an important phone call or is on a deadline. However, one of my goals has been to train the children to play by themselves so that I can either do the dishes, cook dinner, or write. From an early age, they learned to entertain themselves, which is a huge help to me when I need to write during the day.

But it's also important to take time out of your work schedule to play with your children. Each afternoon before the girls nap, we read several stories together.

Throughout the day, I take breaks from housework or writing to sing a song, build a castle, perform a puppet show, or have a tickle-fest.

I've found that by taking breaks and playing with my kids for short chunks of time, I'm able to get more work done because I'm refreshed by the interaction and silly conversation. My children also are more inclined to play again by themselves, knowing that Mommy will be available soon.

Some of the things I've encouraged my children to do by themselves include "reading" or looking at books, playing house, building with blocks, playing doctor/nurse, and listening to music or story CDs in their room. Usually suggesting one of these ideas will net me twenty to thirty minutes of fairly quiet time.

For older children, it's important to let them know when you will be available to interact with them as well. You might want to set aside thirty minutes or so when they arrive home from school to talk about their day, and find out about homework or other activities. Then, while they are off doing homework, perhaps you can squeeze in another hour of work before dinner.

Teaching your children the proper etiquette for interacting

with grown-ups also will help you in your business. From a young age, children can be taught not to interrupt adult conversations on the phone or in-person. Teach them the proper way to address adults, such as using "Mr.," "Mrs.," "Ms.," and "Miss," as well as other polite forms of speech, such as "please," "thank you," "yes, ma'am," and "yes, sir." Older children can learn how to answer the telephone or the door in a professional and polite manner.

Having your children participate in your at-home work, albeit in small ways like answering the phone, can help them to feel more a part of it. This participation can, in time, make them want to help you succeed with their cooperation.

Time with hubby

While you're busy establishing your home-based business, you might be tempted to work every evening after the children are in bed. Except on those rare occasions when you will need to work extra hours because of an especially tight deadline, on a weekly basis you need to set aside time for your husband.

Don't bombard him with your concerns or frustrations right when he walks in the door. Instead, schedule time with him either before or after dinner to talk about your day without the children.

Relax with the love of your life and just enjoy each other's company. As he needs to unwind from his work, so do you.

Regularly have "dates" with your husband. For several years, my husband and I purchased season tickets to a local theater company so that we had at least five or six date nights already on the calendar for the coming year.

If you can't afford a babysitter and an evening out, start a babysitting co-op with other church or neighborhood families. Take turns watching each other's children every couple of months.

Just like with your at-home work, put your dates on the calendar. This will help you not neglect time with your spouse. You both need time together as husband and wife—not as Mommy and Daddy, or as co-workers, or any other hats you wear—in order to build and maintain a strong marriage.

Learning to say 'No'

Keeping a balance between work, home, children, husband, church, family, and friends can be a daunting task. The Christian woman who works from home needs to practice saying "no."

"Trying to keep a balance between my work, home, family, and relationship with God is hard," says Melanie Dobson, a novelist and stay-at-home mother of two preschool children in Portland, Oregon.

"I know God has called me to write, but it's hard some days with everything going on.

"Also, the church seems to put a lot of pressure on women to get overwhelmingly involved, which is impossible to do when you're working and trying to raise a family—at least it's impossible without going over the edge," she continues. "You're requested to do nursery, make meals, attend events, go to playgroups, and attend scrapbooking parties. None of these things are bad by themselves, but women already put enough pressure on themselves. We need to learn how to say 'no' graciously and not feel guilty for doing so. We need to be who God created us to be and not conform to what someone else thinks we need to be."

Before taking on any projects, stop, pray, and wait to say either yes or no. Remember, just because someone asks doesn't mean you have to accept or even answer right away. Discuss each opportunity with your husband, pray before taking on a new task at church or with the children, and always weigh the opportunity against your family's needs and with what God has called you to do. Keep in mind that every opportunity—no matter how good or helpful it may be to others—is not necessarily right for you at that moment.

Time out for me?

It's okay to take time for yourself—the one thing most women have a hard time believing or doing. In fact, you should not feel guilty about having regular "me" time. A woman who goes and goes and goes without taking a break or scheduling regular downtime will soon be a woman on the edge of a breakdown. How can you fulfill your God-given responsibilities if you're running on empty?

The most important aspect of caring for yourself is to spend time each day with the Lord in prayer and devotions. This shouldn't be a hurried reading of Scripture at the breakfast table with one eye on the dog and the other on your toddler (this really hits home with me, too). Cultivating a closer walk with God will enrich your daily work and relationships with your family and clients. Don't neglect this vital aspect of a Christian's daily walk.

Fellowship with other believers also can help keep you on the right track spiritually. Consider joining a small group or weekly Bible study; if you're already part of one, stick with it. Regular intervals of prayer and Bible study with sisters and brothers in Christ can help ease the burdens and magnify the joys of the Christian life. As Matthew records in his Gospel, Jesus wants us to find rest and joy in him:

Then Jesus said, 'Come to me, all of you who are weary and carry heavy burdens, and I will give you rest. Take my yoke upon you. Let me teach you, because I am humble and gentle, and you will find rest for your souls. For my yoke fits perfectly, and the burden I give you is light.' (Matt. 11:28-30)

Keep your body healthy by eating proper meals each day and avoiding too much junk food. Regular exercise invigorates your mental as well as physical well-being. Don't think you have time to add one more thing? Try to rearrange your schedule to allow for exercise. Join a gym or take regular walks. Many fitness centers offer childcare at reduced rates or even for free, too. For example, I try to work out at a gym two to three days a week. I've come to enjoy the solitude and break from the children, and return home renewed and refreshed in body and spirit.

Another aspect of caring for yourself is to take at least a few minutes each day for you. Sit on the front porch for fifteen minutes before the children come home from school, just resting and letting your mind wander. Take a walk with your children. Delay your lunch until the kids are napping to create a little oasis within your day. Spend the half hour before bedtime reading a book instead of watching television. Schedule time to work on a hobby or email friends or family to revitalize your outlook on life. Remember that your well-being is as important as your family's.

Plan regular outings without husband and children. Join a professional group related to your home-based business and attend their meetings. I'm a member of a local writer's group that has bi-monthly meetings, which provide encouragement, fellowship, and inspiration to me as a writer. Meet a friend for coffee once a week or month. Go to the movies or window-shop by yourself every once in a while.

Enlist your husband's assistance in carving out your downtime. Tell him how he can help you enjoy time away from the family. Barter babysitting with other stay-at-home moms for some alone time. You could trade off an afternoon or morning a week, every other week, or once a month to give each woman some time to just be by herself.

If friends and family offer to watch your children or help out with housework when you're on a tight deadline, don't let pride stand in the way of accepting their help.

Several people offered to watch my older children while I was under deadline writing this book, and I gladly took them up on it. Sometimes, you simply cannot do it alone, and making your needs known to other Christian women can be a blessing to them as well as to you.

Taking time for yourself isn't a crime and can restore the balance you need in your roles as wife, mother, and businessperson.

Ask for help from friends and family before you reach the breaking point. Schedule breaks for yourself during the day and week. Date your husband. Play games with your children. Enjoy to the fullest the calling you have as a wife, mother, and worker at home.

Staying in focus

What happens when you're so busy that you just can't focus on anything? The FlyLady offers the following tips[21] for not getting sidetracked.

1. Review the next day's duties before bed.

2. Start your day with your morning routine.

3. Strive to keep your kitchen tidy.

4. Plan your menu by the week or month.

5. Avoid paper piles by sorting mail as soon as it arrives. Have one place for bills. Reconcile your bank statements in a timely manner. Keep circulars, advertisements, and catalogs in one place, and toss the old ones on a regular basis.

6. Schedule a weekly laundry day—then do it.

7. Polish your bathroom and kitchen sinks daily.

8. Make the bed as soon as you get up.

9. Recycle newspapers daily.

10. Put things away as soon as you have finished with them.

11. Unload your car every time you get out.

12. Only drag out enough craft or other projects that you can finish in the time allotted.

13. Establish a routine for your daily chores.

Homeschooling and working

On the surface, homeschooling and at-home employment might not seem like they could peacefully co-exist, but several moms interviewed for this book say that they do homeschool and work from home.

"I have to schedule my day to accomplish all that I have to do," says Angie Dixon, a mother of nine-year-old twins who homeschools and works from home for the family's glass business. "I can homeschool my children, which is a huge advantage for us. Also, my boys and I can travel along with my husband when he goes out of town on business because our arrangement allows us to do that."

The homeschooling mom who works from home has to be especially well-organized so that she can teach her children properly, and devote the time and energy needed to do a good job for her employer and children. Older homeschooled children can self-direct some of their studies at times throughout the day. This can help free up some time that a mom can then use to do her at-home work. 🏠

Melanie Dobson
Novelist

Melanie Dobson has been putting pen to paper from home for seven years—even before she became a mother. "A few months after we got married, my husband took a new job and we moved from Colorado to Virginia," she says. "I'd been wanting to work from home and this was the perfect opportunity."

In Colorado, Melanie was publicity manager for a Christian nonprofit organization. As her own boss she handled media relations for a number of companies and book publishers, coordinating interviews and articles for authors and spokespeople.

"The business grew quickly and my husband quit his job nine months later to go freelance as well (he's a computer animator). I worked around the clock the first few years," says Melanie, adding, "It's easier to start your business before you have kids and have it running when they arrive, instead of trying to start one right after you have a baby." Now living in near Portland, Oregon, they have two daughters, ages three and four.

In 2005, Melanie scaled back her media relations work to

focus more on her fiction writing. Even so, she works twenty to forty hours per week. Thus far, she has written three books, *Latte for One*, *Together for Good*, and *Going for Broke*—all of them published.

While her husband also worked from home, the Dobsons settled on a tag-team approach to caring for their daughters. "I would spend a full day writing and managing my publicity campaigns, while he cared for the girls. Then the next day, I only worked when our kids were sleeping. In six days, we each spent at least forty hours on our freelance work," she says.

Since her husband now has a job at an office, Melanie sometimes needs to rely on others for childcare. "The girls have learned to play by themselves, but when I'm in crunch time, I need help!" Melanie confesses. "I face the constant battle between working and spending time with my girls, and the guilt of not being a mom twenty-four/seven."

She misses having no computer department to call during a crisis and laments the girls' loud crying or playing when she's on a business call. It's tough to deal with interruptions while trying to work, she says.

But the advantages outweigh the negatives: "No commute. Few meetings. Flexible schedule. Always available if my family needs me. And I can pursue the talents and dreams that God gave me. Some women are called to be caregivers around the clock. If I don't have goals or accomplishments outside of care giving (which is a never-ending job), I feel like I'm going crazy," she says.

Angie Dixon
Office Manager

Angie Dixon traded her job as a manager in a retail store for an at-home job managing the office for her husband's glass business more than seven years ago. "I do everything in the office at home for our business," says the Clover, South Carolina-based mom. "I answer the phone, send faxes, do the payroll, take care of the banking, and give estimates."

Being at home during the day enables her to homeschool their nine-year-old twin boys. "I wanted to be home to be more around my children," she says. "I never really dreamed I would actually not be out of the house in the workforce, because I've had a job outside the home since I was twelve. But when the twins came along, they had some health issues that meant they should not be in daycare. So this job has been a positive experience for us in that we've been able to focus more on the priorities of our home and have more control over the structure of our lives."

Angie decided to work from home around the time that the company computerized its records, making the job more streamlined and easier to do from home. "We're much more efficient now and have grown from two employees to twelve," she explains.

She works a minimum of twenty hours a week, but at times logs up to fifty, especially if the project is located in another state. "We relocate the entire business with a job," says Angie. "For example, this past year or so, we were in Colorado for six months, Hawaii for two months, and Charleston, South Carolina, for two months. The boys and I travel with my husband, because homeschooling makes that possible."

In order to fit everything into her day—homeschooling, work, and housework—Angie constantly has to prioritize her schedule. "You definitely have to own your time. Most people don't have this kind of lifestyle of working from home," she says. "Early on, I would get calls from people who thought I had all this free time, and I really had to be deliberate in saying I could have personal calls only during lunch time. I wanted to help but I had to structure my time to get things done."

Her husband has been "amazingly supportive" of her at-home work. "We've both grown a lot in learning to listen to where God's leading us."

The only downside she sees is leaving the job when the work day is over. "When you're on the job outside of the home, it's easier to leave the job at work. With an at-home job, you have to work at not allowing things to rework your scheduled family time."

Toni Friese
Direct Sales Representative

Toni Friese wasn't planning to work from home, but the St. Cloud, Minnesota, mother of a two-year-old found her life out of balance because of all the traveling her job as an event planner required. "I wasn't a good mom, I wasn't a good employee, I wasn't a good wife," she says. An opportunity to become involved with a new direct sales Christian company fell into her lap, and she felt like God was telling her it was time for her to be at home.

The company sells home décor, jewelry, and cards through catalogs and home parties. Toni spends around fifteen hours a week making calls, doing paperwork, and staging parties.

Since she's essentially starting her own business, she's been grateful for her husband and his support from the beginning. "I need to focus on trusting my husband, because he was completely on board with my doing this job," she says.

While Toni's business has not yet brought in enough income to replace her former salary, her husband's faith in her has been invaluable.

"I think it's been a good thing for us in our relationship and I think that it's drawn us closer together. It's nice that this is a faith-based company. Our first goal is growing relationships and developing a closer relationship with God—and that focus has been wonderful for me."

The flexibility allows her to take her son to a play group and for her to run errands in the afternoon. "I'm not depending on somebody else to do those things for me—I have the time to do them myself."

Like most mothers who transition to at-home work, Toni struggles with focusing on what she's doing at that moment and not getting distracted by what else needs to be done. "I could either be doing work stuff or all this home stuff, but when I focus on what I'm doing at that moment, I accomplish more.

However, sometimes it's hard to get motivated to do my work because there's laundry, there's dishes, and there's a book I want to read. It's easy to get sidetracked and there's not as much accountability as there was when I was an event planner. My business is only going to do as well as I put the effort into it. Now, I'm the only one holding myself accountable to be successful," she says.

"But when I was working outside of the home, the balance wasn't there. Now that I'm working from home, I am a better mom and wife."

Rebekah Hammer
University Placement Program Manager

Rebekah Hammer planned on quitting her job as a manager for a university's placement program right before she gave birth to her daughter, but her boss had other ideas. "My boss really wanted me to stay on. I finally agreed because he was willing to take whatever hours I gave him. He was so nice and lenient—just great about it—that I couldn't say no," says this mother of a one-year-old.

She kept her same job title but now manages contracts and university partnership relations instead of managing the entire placement program of six employees and 300-plus students. Rebekah's goal is to work between 10 and 12 hours a week from her Tujunga, California, home, but she usually puts in between seven and eight, given her daughter's schedule.

"At times I feel that I am not working as hard as I could on my job. Before my daughter was born, I would really put in the hours and I did a lot for the company. But now she is my focus and I am torn because I can't do as much for the company as I feel I should. It's not that my boss expects more, just that I feel that I should be giving more," she explains.

Transitioning from working in an office environment to working from home with all the distractions of an infant was hard in the beginning for Rebekah. "My daughter didn't nap very well at first, so I was working 15 minutes here and there. Many days, I didn't have time to clean the house, cook or shower because I was trying to take care of her and still get my work done. Now that she is older and can entertain herself better, I can get a solid hour in without much interruption, which is much better."

One of the hard things for Rebekah is scheduling quiet time for conference calls with an increasingly active baby around. "I have to find a fun and safe place for her to be so that I can pay attention to the call. I don't have a babysitter and it just wouldn't work for my clients to hear a baby in the background."

Her hardest challenge is realizing she cannot be the employee she was before her daughter's birth. "Before her arrival, I could be the manager and take on multiple tasks," Rebekah says. "Now I have to really be honest about what can be put on my plate. I constantly wonder if I am short changing my daughter by not giving her my full attention."

Rebekah misses the energy of the office and feels out of the loop as to what's going on at work since she's not constantly in touch with co-workers. But she's grateful that she can work from home and that her boss is pleased with her work.

"I don't have to work. We could cinch our budget so that we could do without my income," she acknowledges. "But I like to keep my hand in it, so I've continued."

Resources
Books

Boundaries with Kids
by Dr. Henry Cloud and Dr. John Townsend

Children Who Do Too Little
by Patricia Sprinkle

*Elbows Off the Table, Napkin in the Lap, No Video Games During Dinner:
The Modern Guide to Teaching Children Good Manners*
by Carol McD. Wallace

*The Gift of Good Manners: A Parent's Guide to Raising Respectful, Kind,
Considerate Children*
by Peggy Post and Cindy Post Senning, Ed.D.

*How Clean Is Your House?: Hundreds Of Handy Tips
to Make Your Home Sparkle*
by Kim Woodburn and Aggie MacKenzie

*How to Say No Without Feeling Guilty: And Say Yes to More Time, and
What Matters Most to You*
by Patti Breitman and Connie Hatch

Learning To Say No: Establishing Healthy Boundaries
by Carla Wills-Brandon

Once a Month Cooking
by Mary Beth Lagerborg and Mimi Wilson

One Thing at a Time: 100 Simple Ways to Live Clutter-Free Every Day
by Cindy Glovinsky

Raising Adults: Getting Kids Ready for the Real World
by Jim Hancock

Sink Reflections
by Marla Cilley, The FlyLady

Online

Chores for children checklist
www.printablechecklists.com/checklist11.shtml
Provides printable forms and an article about assigning chores to children.

FlyLady
www.flylady.net
Provides tips, tools, and encouragement for keeping your house in order.

Mad About Manners
www.schoolofprotocol.com
The article "A Lifeskills Approach to Teaching Manners," by Cathleen Hanson and Carol Campbell Haislip, provides tips on training children.

Saving Dinner
www.savingdinner.com
Provides tips and recipes for making cooking easy and delicious.

Conclusion

Where Do You go From Here?

This book is only the starting point for your own work-from-home business. Use it as a guide along every step of your journey to at-home employment. Be inspired by the stories of other Christian women from all walks of life who share similar struggles, dreams, frustrations, and successes of working from home. Remember that we all come from different backgrounds, different situations, different vocations—and that we're all at different points on this journey.

Some of you reading this book will decide to postpone working from home because it's not the right fit for you and your family situation at this time. If that's the case, don't be discouraged. Remember that waiting for the right time—God's time—is always better than forcing things to happen prematurely.

Some of you will find unexpected roadblocks at points along the way that might frustrate or dishearten you. Keep praying, keep pressing forward, keep evaluating your motives, and you will soon find your way. It might take longer than you anticipated, but embrace the opportunity that delays offer to refine your work-from-home idea and address any potential difficulties that pop up.

Some of you will find it hard to transition from staying at home and not working (with or without children) to starting at-home employment. The tugs of housework and other responsibilities can be strong, even when you know you have other work to accomplish. Having to adhere to a tighter schedule or giving up some activities and free time can be tiring or annoying, but if you truly feel this is the new path you need to trod, with God's help, you will prevail and succeed.

Some of you will discover right away that working from home is easier and more fulfilling and enjoyable than you initially thought it might be. You might even wonder why you took so long to take that step.

Whatever your current situation, wherever you are in the work-from-home process—just starting out, in the midst of it, or an established veteran—be encouraged.

You are not alone.

The number of Christian women using their God-given talents, abilities, and gifts for at-home employment is growing every day.

Go forth with confidence, knowing that you possess the ability to start, maintain and succeed at a home-based business.

Acknowledgements

I am grateful for the assistance many provided in the shaping and writing of this book. Most especially, I thank my husband, Christian, without whom this book never would have come to be. His encouragement, sound advice, and willingness to take on additional responsibilities at home (and for not sighing too loud when his question of "What's for dinner?" was met with "Dinner? We have to eat tonight?") were invaluable.

I also sincerely appreciate the willingness of Betsy DeMarco, Melanie Dobson, Elizabeth Spencer, and Karla Vernon to read all or part of my manuscript and offer both positive and critical feedback. My fellow writers at Capitol Christian Writers provided spiritual and moral support when sorely needed.

And, finally, I thank all the women who shared their struggles, inspiration, and insights about working from home. It is their stories that give this book its heart.

Sarah Hamaker
2008

Endnotes

1 Jones, T. Foster. "Mom's the Word." *The Costco Connection,* May 2007, p. 22.

2 One note about at-home work and home-based businesses: I'm defining at-home work or at-home employment as work that you do for one specific company, or for client companies who contract with you to perform short-term or long-term projects. When I refer to home-based business, I mean a business that you started and run personally; these businesses generally sell products or services to the general populace.

3 Burton, Linda, Janet Dittmer, and Cheri Loveless. *What's a Smart Woman Like You Doing At Home?* Revised Edition. Vienna, Virginia: Mothers At Home, 1992. p. 111.

4 Elmer, Vickie. "Mothers Superior." *The Washington Post,* May 11, 2007.

5 Ibid.

6 Frey, Jennifer. "The Other 364 Days of Mom's Year." *The Washington Post,* May 8, 2005.

7 Jones, p. 22.

8 Gibson, Mary Bass. *The Family Circle Book of Careers at Home.* Chicago: Cowles Book Company, Inc., 1971.

9 *Costco Connection,* p. 23.

10 Klein, Karen. "The Face of Entrepreneurship in 2017." *BusinessWeek,* January 31, 2007, www.businessweek.com/print/smallbiz/content/jan2007/sb20070131_094012.htm/ accessed 4/21/08.

11 Venker, Suzanne. *7 Myths of Working Mothers.* Dallas: Spence Publishing Company, 2004, p. 6.

12 Burkett, Larry. *Women Leaving the Workplace.* Chicago: Moody Press, 1995, p. 14.

13 Burkett, p. 198.

14 Venker, p. 158.

15 Venker, p. 50.

16 www.bls.gov/news.release/ecopro.nr.htm/ U.S. Department of Labor/ accessed 3/14/08.

17 Employment growth will continue to be concentrated in the service-providing sector of the economy, the U.S Department of Labor (DOL) predicts. Industry sectors adding the most jobs (8.1 million) are professional and business services, and healthcare and social assistance. Overall, the labor force is growing more slowly due to "aging and retiring baby boomers"—which will also create more job openings in the future, the DOL reports.

18 Singletary, Michelle. "Swindler's List: Dieters, Debtors and You." *The Washington Post,* November 8, 2007.

19 Klein, Karen. "Best Home-Based Business Ideas." *BusinessWeek,* January 10, 2007. http://www.businessweek.com/smallbiz/content/jan2007/sb20070110_343896.htm/ BusinessWeek, accessed 4/21/08.

20 www.irs.gov/businesses/small/article/0,,id=115045,00.html/ accessed 4/21/08.

21 Adapted from the FlyLady's "Tips for Not Getting Sidetracked," www.flylady.net/pages/FLYingLessons_Tips.asp/ accessed 4/21/08.

Sarah Hamaker loves to hear from her readers!
You can go to her website

www.SarahHamaker.com

to blog, catch up on her schedule, read her
newsletter, and send email to her.

Sarah Hamaker is available to speak to your group about
how to work from home. You can contact her through her
website, above.

Media Requests: To interview Sarah about this book,
work-from-home trends, or how to begin working from
home, please contact DPL Press, Inc., at 562 634-6750,
business hours, Pacific time.

Thank You!

Index

Z

MORE TITLES FROM
DPL PRESS, INC.

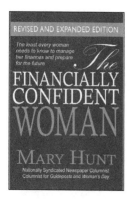

**The Financially
Confident Woman**
978-1-9345080-1-5

In Stores NOW!
$14.95

**The Frugal
Duchess**
978-1-9345080-0-8

In Stores June '08
$14.95

**No Fear
Entrepreneur**
978-0-9760791-6-3

Coming SOON!

Tiptionary 2
978-0-9760791-5-6
In Stores NOW
$14.95

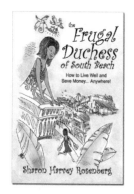

**Debt-Proof
Living**
978-0-9760791-1-8
In Stores NOW
$16.99

**Debt-Proof Your
KIDS**
978-09760791-4-9
In Stores NOW
$14.99

Available wherever fine books are sold or call 800 550-3502

Sign up to get Mary Hunt in your email box ... every weekday! ... It's **FREE!**

Subscribe to the FREE *Everyday Cheapskate* email and join Mary's daily newspaper column readers who count on their daily fix from Mary Hunt ...

- ◆ Tips—lots of tips!
- ◆ Reader mail
- ◆ Questions and answers
- ◆ Money-management tools
- ◆ Financial advice
- ◆ Product reviews
- ◆ Success stories
- ◆ Motivation
- ◆ Inspiration
- ◆ HOPE ... every day!

Remember it's **FREE!** ... Sign up at

www.EverydayCheapskate.com

See you tomorrow and every day!